TECHNOLOGIES
OF ROMANCE

PART I

Paul O'Kane

TECHNOLOGIES OF ROMANCE – PART I

Preface by Howard Caygill

Illustration by Luna Sun

Published by eeodo

"The act of reaching for a lighter or a spoon is familiar routine, yet we hardly know what really goes on between hand and metal, not to mention how this fluctuates with our moods".

— Walter Benjamin

CONTENTS

THANK YOU

First, thanks to my skilled, inventive and conscientious eeodo colleagues, Bada Song & Barnaby Lambert, with whom it is always adventurous, occasionally nerve-wracking, but ultimately fulfilling to work. This, fourth eeodo publication has my name on the cover but is in so many ways the outcome of our special creative relationship and precious friendship. Thanks to all students and ex-students of the *Technologies of Romance* seminar (previously *The B-Team* seminar) at Central St Martins College, UAL. Many thanks to Graham Ellard and Debi Kenny (also CSM, UAL) who guided me regarding internal research funding, and to all colleagues at CSM, UAL, particularly Kate Love, Jon Cairns, Alex Schady and Mick Finch. Thanks to all my AICA UK and AICA International colleagues. On behalf of eeodo I thank Luna Sun for her drawing and patience with our design process. Thanks to Tony Yard and Scott House at London College of Communication (UAL) for friendly advice and skills in litho printing and folding. Thanks to Peter at J. Muir for binding and Bill at G.F Smith regarding papers. eeodo thank everyone involved in hosting, funding, attending and participating in our launch events. Particular thanks go to Howard Caygill (also for his charming preface here), Kim Longinotto, Sophie Mayer and Maria Walsh, who all agreed to contribute to our Whitechapel Gallery symposium launch. Thanks also to our Whitechapel host, Gareth Evans. Finally, thank you to anyone reading this. eeodo books are the culmination of an adventure in ideas and the composition of creative interactions between materials, minds, hands and machines, always aiming to translate the elusive, complex and speculative into something substantial, coherent and of enduring value.

DEDICATION

I was recently reminded of the phenomenon of *Radio Caroline*, a pirate radio station hurriedly contrived to fill a demand in 1960s Britain for new pop music to be freely available on national airwaves. I recall now that, as a child, one of my three older brothers conveyed his excitement about it to me. He may have also indoctrinated me into what I now call *Technologies of Romance* when, during a family holiday on the Norfolk coast, he took me to a local café complete with jukebox. The device itself, which I had never seen before, was magical (they still are), and the sound it produced — once a coin dropped into its slot, a selection was made, and its needle touched a spinning 7" record — proved unforgettable. On that occasion Jack Bruce's deep, rich bassline to Cream's *Badge* (1969) cruised out of the speakers and filled the otherwise nearly empty café with instant pleasure and heaps of cool.

I have to thank the same brother for enthusiastically introducing all his younger siblings to his first battery operated transistor radio, his first portable cassette recorder, his first record player, his first *stereo* record player, his first headphones, his first album featuring explicit stereo panning (*Led Zeppelin I*), his first slide projector etc. The same brother brought the first electric guitar into the house, and as I set out to write this book I appreciate all I owe to him, and thus dedicate the following to the illustrious and irrepressible poet, songwriter, hard working, generous and all round helpful Steve O'Kane.

Nevertheless, that dedication might seem unfair to another of my influential older brothers who brought the first (male) long hair into the house, along with the first acoustic guitar, the first Bob Dylan, Joni Mitchell, and Simon & Garfunkel records, along with the first maps, compass, camping stove, sleeping bag, tent, touring bicycle, YHA and RSPB membership, guides to Britain's public footpaths and an ambitious plan to obtain a collapsible canoe. He was also the first to leave the family home and travel across the country by hitching rides, driven by some apparently irrepressible and adventurous nomadic wanderlust that marked out his generation, and which is still shaping and motivating his retirement. This book is then also dedicated to Mike O'Kane, another mighty spirit, great influence, kind, generous brother, and life guide.

It would be reductive, inaccurate and unfair however to line–up one of these mentors on the technologies side of my influences and the other on the romance side, as they both, in their own ways inform, influence and inspire the contents of this book more comprehensively and roundly than any such dualism might infer. In fact, the rich array of their combined and diverse contributions, listed above, points to one of the central aims of this book i.e. a wish to pluralise, historicise and synthesise notions of technology and romance in such a way as to draw the two into a new union.

PREFACE

TECHNOLOGIES OF ROMANCE

While waiting for Paul in the reception of a hotel near the Gare du Nord, I idly pick up one of the five copies of today's *Le Figaro* carefully arranged on a glass table. Bored by it all I languidly rustle the pages until arriving at the photograph of a knapped stone axe–head illustrating an interview with a paleo–technologist on some recent archaeological finds in Kenya. Have I got this right? I read again, more slowly. Yes, the tools recently discovered precede the oldest human remains by over two hundred thousand years.

I consider the options. Perhaps these are the tools of a lost humanity whose bones are now entirely dispersed in the earth, or...? I slip into a reverie of a distant future where crushed smart phones, pulverised cars and the oxidised traces of the Eiffel Tower re–emerge somewhere in a desert, occupied by today's Antartica, as a thin geological strata — all that is left of all that we ever did. What was Jan Zalasiewicz's estimate in *The World After Us* — all of humanity and its technological efforts as a sediment layer of a hundredth of an inch?

Outside the cars passing on the Boulevard du Magenta slow down and blur as the seas return to Paris and its sounds, airs, its very fabric resolve into an emission of bubbles emitted for a few seconds from the sea bed, unnoticed and insignificant. But all the same, why does the thought that technology will stand witness for humanity after their utter dispersal only contribute to its romance, and why is this survival story more comforting than the other solution to the puzzle of the anachronous tools, the one that holds that humans did not invent technology, but technology humans?

In this story we are an effect and not the cause of technology and accordingly we came later because we came after… And what if we were not just a by–product but a romance of technology, a toy contrived to amuse and comfort itself during its slow gestation? Then, all that would remain to be contemplated in a technological future would be the stratigraphic evidence of its romantic childhood and adolescence, traces of humanity as one of the childish things it put behind itself when coming of age. Buried in the earth, or carried across the universe in the spectral lines of our transmitted light, humanity and technology become odd and strangely synchronous fossils.

I look up hopefully as the automatic doors of the hotel open with a sigh, but it's still not Paul. I carefully fold and put back the newspaper fully resolved — when he finally gets here I will tell him he must update the Kant epigraph at the conclusion of his book thus:

'Two things fill the mind with ever increasing admiration and awe, the more often and steadily we reflect on them: the starry heavens above and the ground beneath our feet.'

Howard Caygill

INTRODUCTION

Now it returns, a gift from the past, a memory of a cold, bright, late winter — early spring day in nineteen ninety–something. The Broadgate Centre, London. The whole sky shone over and into me, a benign blue force eradicating the distance between myself and heaven. A suited, booted and necktied Japanese businessman, ice–skating backwards in wide, lazy circles, hands non-chalantly clasped behind his back. I felt slightly high on what was then, for me, a rare dose of strong black coffee, drunk from a wide brimming cup. Experiencing some kind of *satori* I noted anew how life depends upon ma-terials and things, ice–skates and coffee, suits and ties, just as much as any cerebral or spiritual journey I might be on (searching for alternatives, a future, a way out). The Japanese business man, so centered, so calm and well–adjusted to this capitalist city, skated backwards, oblivious to cares, time, aims or goals, enjoying a little lunchtime luxury, lightly scoring circles in a smooth disk of ice, a grown–up's toy installed near the heart of the financial district, which (they say) makes this world go around.

But why mix academic and memoir writing, presence and past, words and pictures? Following on from my pre-vious **eeodo** publication *Where Is That Light Now?* (2014) I wanted to develop certain strategies initiated there. The notion of intratextuality is used again here, and image and text (artfully interacting in all **eeodo** publications to date) deepen their relationship. Academic and memoir writing once again attempt to present a holistic presenta-tion of a life and a concept, sensed and theorised, lived and written, felt and thought.

Is romance a dirty word? How can we define technology? In writing this book, and in teaching a seminar of the same name, I have only warmed to my two, apparently incongruous keywords, and continue to find their interplay both fractious and productive. Here, technology is never restricted to modern devices and, projected into distant history, proves an unusually expansive concept. Meanwhile, far from encouraging any simplistic or conservative re–evaluation of romance and Romanticism, both are intended as mild provocations. Romanticism may have always been an affront to modern art, and the border between the two is repeatedly tended here. Romanticism, applied to nationality, has a fascist past and enduring fascist potential (of increasing concern to the political landscape as I write). Nevertheless, Romanticism also informed the revolutionary spirit that led us to today's bourgeois democracy and which might be called upon again to rejuvenate our cherished narrative of social progress.

There is surely a canon of gendered critique responding to the concept of romance (I am thinking of an expert such as Marina Warner) and I apologise in advance if this has not been explicitly addressed in what follows. Partly to redress this shortcoming, the symposium organised to launch this book invites several leading feminist spokeswomen (all also experts in moving image) to respond to our title and theme.

Recently I met an editor, just retiring from a long career with a leading arts publisher, who warned me of the folly of trying to translate a successful seminar into a successful publication. He insisted that writing, and the book format, could never capture and relay the experience of a room alive with enthusiastically interacting voices and ideas. Nevertheless, as the book evolved, in terms of writing, illustration, design and production, myself and my **eeodo** colleagues endeavoured to shape its characteristics and values in ways that retain something of the seminar's tone, content and enjoyment, or at least to compensate for their loss in translation from one format to another. I set out by writing in response to a seminar recording but increasingly used unaided memory, until the writing began to claim its own form and impose its own priorities.

The Central St Martins BAFA *Technologies of Romance* seminar (and *The B–Team* seminar from which it grew) has been one of the outstanding experiences of my art teaching career. Its agenda, initially not much more than a hunch, has proven valuable and relevant to an annually changing cohort of about thirty students. Exploring the seminar's theme has also allowed me to clarify the very heart of my own lifelong interest in art, thought, history and culture.

Each week, and each year of the seminar, we discursively found our way to particular areas of concentration so that once we found ourselves collectively inhabiting the ruins of an abandoned Second Life project, while on another occasion we considered the design of 'Alone, But Not Lonely'–style solo seating units in contemporary campus cafés. More recently we meditated on the idiosyncratic technology of the humble postcard, its romantic, Romanticist, narrative, historical, and technological implications.

This book has never aspired to be a comprehensive representation of the contents of the seminar. I always knew that there would be significant omissions, not least because the seminar has accumulated a large archive of related ideas and materials over a period of ten years. Furthermore, the act of writing, which must be allowed to find its own form, plus pressures of design, manufacture and dissemination, conspired to produce this selective, but hopefully focused and coherent reflection.

While the widest range and history of technologies are always entertained, in both the seminar and in preparation for this book, I concede that personal passions for photography, literature, cinema and philosophy have informed its content. However, substantial materials, set aside for subsequent possible volumes, promise to eventually redress this balance and reveal the broadest potential of our theme.

Both seminar and book have consistently attended to current technologies, but it was always my aim to relativise the newest technologies according to a long history of technologies. Thinking historically, I thus sought to de–mythologise so–called new technologies, to a point whereby students and readers might feel better able to respond to them critically, and not just complacently.

While striving to maintain a contemporary focus, the seminar, perhaps inevitably, confirmed that it is the primary responsibility of one generation (my own) to bequeath to younger students — most of whom qualify as so–called 'digital natives' — not so much canonic content as (perhaps more importantly) a vigilant, creative and critical approach to life and culture. Students, and all readers of this book are thus encouraged to contribute their own particular knowledge, cultural perspective, experience and expertise, in updating, applying and extending the ways and means proffered here as a kind of tool kit with which to explore art, history and culture. To illuminate this point with an example, computer games are barely mentioned in what follows, despite the fact that my (limited) knowledge of them leads me to believe they would provide a fertile focus for discussion of their relationship and relevance to our themes of romance, narrative, technologies and Romanticism.

At a crucial point in the progress of this project, the **eeodo** team decided to reduce the book's scale by half. This confirmed the present volume as Part I of a planned pair or possible series of books. While the book's dedication, the opening paragraph of this introduction, as well as its illustrations may all promise to focus upon technologies in terms of discreet objects, gadgets, tools and toys, I have in fact set aside, for a subsequent publication, a swathe of words related to that fertile theme. Here, as this book gradually found its own identity, I may have produced a more historical and abstract text, but one on which I hope to be able to confidently build in a subsequent volume, or volumes, free to pursue various sub–themes drawn from the rich array of materials and ideas that have emerged during the history of the seminar.

As with previous **eeodo** publications, an intratextual self–reflexivity influenced this book's evolution, nurtured with the aim of producing, not just an academic text but a roundly considered artist's book, valued for its material properties as much as any intellectual and literary content. *Technologies of Romance* may haunt the established academic territories of new media and technoromanticism; of Romanticism as an art historical or literary discipline; or of romance, narrative and storytelling as aspects of literature, life–writing or psychology, however, it has never consciously aspired to contribute to any arena more specific than that of art, culture, ideas and book–making.

To make a book at all in the twenty first century is a questionable proposition. It might be considered an anachronistic vehicle, burdened with mass and materiality and tied to costly and cumbersome industrial processes. Nevertheless, the **eeodo** team have once again carefully considered here how this historical format might continue to further the ancient and noble tradition of taking responsibility and care for the dissemination of art and ideas — a concern for conscientiousness that may be of increasing importance at a time threatened by an increase in barbarism.

The chapters that follow are both united and divided, heterogeneous and homogeneous. Each forms as autonomous a piece as it was capable of becoming given the schedule imposed by the book's manufacture. Sometimes a chapter clearly continues from that which precedes it, but hopefully all allude to each other in less linear fashion, by means of echoes and refrains.

While the contents of the chapters strive to compliment,

the style in which they are written varies, sometimes swayed by their particular subject matter, and occasionally by the intervention of a memoir–like, more subjective voice, already heard at the beginning of this introduction.[1] For much of the text a more objective and academic 'we' or 'our' tends to supplant the possibly more romantic 'I'. However, sophisticated twenty first century readers will hopefully concur that this 'I' and this 'we' may be construed as both equally performative and equally authoritative. Therefore, given a holistic and relativist ethos, no hierarchy need be imposed upon these mixed voices.

Even as tone, content and perspective may vary, hopefully this book remains loyal to its key terms and thus maintains a consistent, if necessarily oblique enquiry. Nevertheless, alongside romance, Romanticism, and technologies, two related terms that consistently arise (as almost inevitable ramifications) are narrative and storytelling.

Certain personae, drawn from the history of the arts, also make brief, sometimes repeated entrances on the stage of history assembled here. They include Don Quixote, Scheherazade, Othello and Charlie Chaplin. Meanwhile a personal pantheon of writers and commentators, accompanied by a selection of favoured and familiar texts (as featured in the seminar), brings together reference or allusion to Walter Benjamin, Charles Baudelaire, Jean Baudrillard, Hito Steyerl, Tanya Harrod, Mary Shelley, Richard Holmes, John Clare and William Shakespeare,

---

1. A similar mix of objective and subjective voices can be found in previous **eeodo** publications: *Cash or Smash* (2015), *"I'm Alone, But Not Lonely"* (2016), and *Where Is That Light Now?* (2014).

augmented by momentary appeals to Friedrich Nietzsche, Immanuel Kant and Martin Heidegger.

The order of chapters was never intended to infer a chronology, though in early drafts later chapters did gravitate towards increased discussion of contemporary technology. Contrary to this tendency, a valid argument grew for editing–out much contemporary observation from a book that aspires to make an enduring contribution (as a historical perspective on its theme, and as itself a work of art) and which therefore wishes to avoid blurring its purpose with those of journalism, blogs or social networks. Hopefully sufficient contemporary reference and relevance remains for this book to make a valuable, if idiosyncratic contribution to current issues and debates.

Finally, along with much material set–aside for subsequent publications, a longer, more wayward, but perhaps more detailed introduction has been supplanted by this more concise summary. Hopefully no information essential to the satisfactory experience of what follows has been lost. Ultimately of course, it may be preferable for the reader to embark on this adventure — as might any qualified Romantic — relatively *un*prepared.

THINKING
HISTORICALLY

To consider the present critically, questionably, vigilantly and speculatively is to live and think historically. To think historically might mean, not so much to concentrate on the past as to perceive the present as a peculiar and particular outcome of the past which is also partly informed by our image of the future.

Heidegger seemed to perceive technology as a form of inexorable and immanent historical agency, a manifestation of man's insatiable sense of empowerment and ascendancy. Romance, we might argue, is a term equally infused with historical agency.[1] To live in the past, or to think of the past as a better time than this, is often deemed romantic. However, maintaining a positive view of the future may also be regarded as evidence of an optimistically romantic spirit, one that insists things can be better than they presently are. The modern, revolutionary spirit that led us to democracy emerged in part from a Romantic tradition according to which we not only came to marvel at nature and, contemporaneously, at scientific and technological possibility, but also, and perhaps consequently, fostered an atmosphere of optimistic speculation regarding social change.

A walk around two or three adjacent rooms in London's National Portrait Gallery, themed according to the Georgian epoch in England, reveals portraits of Thomas Paine and Mary Wollstonecraft, as well as history paintings marking the abolition of slavery and the 1832 Reform Act (with its increased suffrage). These rub shoulders with

1.   Heidegger, M. (1977).

portraits of McAdam, Ricardo, Davey, Jenner and Herschel, who in turn mingle with Blake, Byron, Wordsworth, Keats, the Shelleys and John Clare.[2] This juxtaposition seems to provide evidence of the particular interplay of Romanticism, technology and social change informing the emergence of modernity, and to which this book attends.

Technology has as much to do with the past as the present or future. Meanwhile, romance may be as futural as Romanticism is apparently historical. Technology, in common parlance, generally signifies innovation, often pointing to the latest technology as a breach with or exception to history. We feel fortunate to inhabit and enjoy the particular technologies of our time as they even seem to summarise or emblematise our age, and yet even the newest technology cannot escape its connection to the longest history. Thus, novelty inadvertently and perhaps paradoxically invokes the past, surreptitiously delivering history into our midst in new guise.

Occasionally in Walter Benjamin's work, e.g. his writing on Kafka, *The Work Of Art In The Age of Mechanical Reproduction* essay, or *The Storyteller*,[3] we gain a sense that, despite his enthusiasm for the *avant–garde* it is perhaps tradition that most deeply concerns him. While Benjamin seems ahead of the curve in valuing photography and cinema, and in championing progressive artists, beneath

2. Crane, D., Hebron, S. & Woof, R. (Entries). (2002).

3. Benjamin, W. (1968). pp.83–109 (*The Storyteller*). pp. 111–145 (*Franz Kafka on the Tenth Anniversary of His Death*). pp. 217–251 (*The Work of Art in The Age of Mechanical Reproduction*).

this passion for innovation he is concerned with finding a means by which to respect, protect and deliver tradition into and through modernity, while nevertheless allowing modernity to play itself out unhindered by any crudely conservative function.

Crucially, Benjamin does not sacrifice the old and the new on the altar of a crude dualism, nor by means of dogmatic dialectics, but consistently finds ways to remind us of the possible continuity, contiguity and contingency of the old and the new; we might even say their indifference to the imposition of any traumatic and divisive dualism. Thus the ancient takes modern form and is never left behind — even in the great gold rush for modernity. Meanwhile, modernity is revealed as the emerging surface of the ancient, the new as the constant rebirth of a long tradition of invention and possibility. The newest technologies prove capable of awakening our interest in history, even as they appear to have us enraptured in a timeless state of fascination.

Today, our engagement with the virtual and the digital promises to transport us to an *a*historical realm, the only apparent history on our laptop screens being the searches *cached* by our browsers and which — unlike certain other forms of history — are easy to erase without any corresponding sense of loss or irresponsibility. Our digital history, a relatively new, immaterial form, might nevertheless lead us to consider the extent to which Historical Materialism (the doctrine Marx adapted from the thought of Hegel and which Benjamin playfully challenged in his *Theses on a Philosophy of History*[4] was defined and determined by the technology and relative materiality of Marx's own time, thus suggesting an understanding of history as inevitably and intrinsically 'placed' in the world (Heidegger's concepts of dwelling and *Dasein* are germane).[5] If so, changing technologies and the changing value of materiality itself may ask us today to entertain the notion of an *a*historical *im*materialsm or perhaps a Historical *Virtualism*.

The new technologies of our time may have kindled a compensatory historical affection for what Benjamin, in his essay on Surrealism, called "the outmoded". A student today might carry a retro or vintage re–issue Polaroid camera along with the technically superior digital camera mounted on their smartphone. Meanwhile, the same student's tutor might avidly re–collect vinyl records favoured in their youth, while nevertheless streaming all the music they need via an online provider. Thus, while we are rocketed into the future by microprocessors, we rescue and are rescued by a long history of technologies, relativising their respective value and purpose.

History is neither empty[6] nor inherently virtuous, but constantly used, abused, and filled, even strategically stuffed and padded for political ends. As we load ethical demands, narratives, and causality onto history so history

---

4. Benjamin, W. (1968). pp. 253–264.

5. Heidegger, M. (1993) and Heidegger, M. (2001).

6. Benjamin, W. (1968). pp. 253–264. "Empty time" is a phrase used repeatedly by Benjamin in his *Theses On A Philosophy of History* to refute the casual notion of history as something abstract, immaterial or transcendent.

makes demands upon us, asserting a special influence that requires us to live our lives more conscientiously and take our actions more seriously. When significant technological and social change is simmering around us, and perhaps especially at such times, it may be our sense of history (and histories large and small), that best expresses our faith in a shared human project and which might therefore help guide us safely into the future. Thus Walter Benjamin might have justified the time he spent, during a trip to revolutionary 1920s Moscow, searching for handmade toys.[7] He thereby seemed to demonstrate that the value and importance of collecting and treasuring the past (and particularly the past as curious, idiosyncratic or extraordinary) should not be demeaned, underestimated or considered contrary to revolutionary aspirations.

Can technology, as a form of progressive narrative, ever fail or be fundamentally questioned, as might other paradigmatic narratives? We might embrace a model of post–modernism but it may be more difficult to ever see ourselves as post–technological. Heidegger seems to expand our notion of technology to mean something with which we have always contended and always will.[8] Given this definition it becomes difficult *not* to discern technology as something immanent and all–pervasive. Technology begins to seem an omnipresent force, a universal cult, a power in which we *must* believe and to which we regularly and ultimately defer. Even if human beings are not the only technological species, humanity

7.   Benjamin, W. (1985).

8.   Heidegger, M. (1977).

regards itself as defined by its technologies. We use our technological development to legitimate, understand and provide evidence for ourselves as superior, extraordinarily dynamic creatures. We might equally trumpet our exceptional language, art, aptitude for spiritual reflection or intricately reflexive consciousness, and yet technology, in the broadest sense that we can deploy the term, might significantly inform all of these admirable attributes, thus playing the most significant part of all in forming what we think of as our humanity. Seventeenth century Christian philosopher Blaise Pascal, for example, rigorously investigated his ability to believe in God and partly resolved his dilemma by means of an appeal to the technology of actions and gestures associated with the performance of his faith.[9]

While we may barely comprehend or confront the unpalatable implications of our natural evolution we enjoy the proud narrative of our technological progress, which seems to distance and distinguish us from nature and even from our own nature. However, if it is true that technology is somehow other to and at odds with nature then this should perhaps help define what technology is? From whence does it emerge? Is it a kind of intelligence? A way of acting *on* the world that is perhaps less natural than simply living *in* and *with* the world? To resort briefly to biblical allegory, we might ask, is technology perhaps the snake in the garden of nature, the apple, or the act of reaching out for and taking of fruit that could be allowed to ripen and fall of its own volition? Does the root of

9. Pascal, B. (1995). p. 247.

technology thus lie in shamefully utilitarian, willful and exploitative acts which benefit ourselves at the expense of our environment? Perhaps at this point we could also consult Australian aboriginal peoples who apparently have no word for, nor concept of 'progress' and who see their fundamental role and aim as conserving the earth as it was at the moment of its creation. Perhaps *they* are non–technological? But then, even the briefest consideration of their lifestyle reveals this to be untrue.[10]

The authors and texts to whom and to which we refer in what follows, share a tendency to think historically. Walter Benjamin looms largest among them and remains an exemplary figure, scrutinising his times in terms of technological impact while considering various ways in which history and humanity might appropriately respond. The first quarter of the twentieth century confronted humanity with manifold forms of unprecedented technological change, and Benjamin scrupulously considered what this meant for society, history, thought, and art. He tried to understand how modernity might be handled, endured, exploited and utilised by artists who (as Brian Eno stated in a recent lecture) are often the first to experiment with new technologies and who may therefore be responsible for humanising those technologies.[11]

As the final chapters of this book suggest, artists can turn

---

10. See Wade Davis' review of *The World Until Yesterday* by Jared Diamond in The Guardian (9th January, 2013). www.theguardian.com/books/2013/jan/09/history-society (see p. 151 of this book for full citation).

11. See Brian Eno's BBC Music *John Peel Lecture*. www.bbc.co.uk/programmes/p033smwp

crisis into craft or make technological shock less alien and ugly, partly by progressively synthesising and accommodating new technologies within pre–existing frames of reference. Recall that Benjamin's scope incorporated not only a prescient and precocious critical analysis of cinema but the championing of popular cultural icon Charlie Chaplin, surely the biggest star of Benjamin's era, and one who — we might say — played a significant part in successfully humanising one of the most pervasive new technologies influencing his own time — cinema.

Just as teenagers in Bronx projects would one day come to adapt their uncles' record decks and vinyl collections to invent their very own, startlingly innovative yet simultaneously archival Hip Hop music, so Chaplin effectively adapted the long histories of clowning and sentimental storytelling to the new technology with which he was confronted. He thus played a part in healing the technological ruptures of his own time while bringing laughter to millions caught–up in seething and unseemly socio–economic turmoil. While innovating, Chaplin also repaired and extended tradition, and thus we see again that modernity demands, not only the new but new vehicles and new interpreters by means of which to bend, guide, enable and perpetuate tradition in its every moment of crisis and rebirth.

As Benjamin and his Frankfurt School[12] associates demonstrated, living, thinking and seeing historically allows us

---

12. The Frankfurt School is a school of social theory and philosophy founded in Germany in the inter–war period with the aim of developing new methods of exploring, challenging and explicating modern, capitalist society.

to value, as simultaneously exceptional and as linked in a historical chain, that which is 'right under our noses'. According to their urgent interest and influence, the habitual and everyday are rendered, not only extraordinary but — more crucially — as *arbitrary*, never simply given or destined, never (as the 1930s Gershwin song phrased it) "... *necessarily so*".

By stopping to consider an apparently modest, ordinary, man–made artefact as historically significant, we are invited to consider not only its social value and historical meaning but also its technological evolution, and thus, by implication, myriad objects or variations that might have evolved in its place, or other ways in which it might have technologically matured. The merest paper cup or paperclip[13] thus becomes worthy of historical scrutiny once we hesitate before it, consider its peculiarities, past and possible future curled–up within its current condition. Any object, event, or encounter becomes evidence of the historical flux within which we ourselves — our life, our society — are immanently and inexorably embroiled. The everyday is thus infused with the potential to encounter the mysterious value of that secular mystique nominated by Benjamin as a "profane illumination".

The political and revolutionary potential of thinking historically lies in *not* taking for granted the current form or value of any object, image or encounter but rather regarding all as critical and questionable expressions of

---

13. Stone, O. (Director). (1987). In the movie *Wall Street*, the lead character, Gekko, played by Michael Douglas, refers to a paperclip while explaining the workings of free market capitalism to a relative novice.

history. But what is the relationship between history and technology? Marx materialised Hegel's more abstract and spiritual interpretation of history, but Heidegger's image of technology seems to be an immanent condition. Technology has a narrative of its own that manifests change as and in embodied forms of evident progress. Is technology then a spirit, or firmly located in materiality? Benjamin strives to find a convincing way, his *own* way, to synthesise or move–on from any given religious, scientific, Hegelian or Marxist understandings of history. We too may be able to synthesise, reconcile or homogeonise the relationship between history and technology; between Heidegger, Hegel and Marx; and between spirit and material, by positing a material history unfolded by technology as that material history's irrepressible agency of change. Here technology is also synthesised with its own inherent narrativity — what we might call its own romance.

Photographer Robert Burley provided a concrete example of thinking historically in his 2012 publication *The Disappearance of Darkness*. This collection of the author's own photographs records the collapse and destruction of the chemical or analog photography industry that had enabled and sustained Burley's career as a professional photographer.[14] Here however, he made carefully executed analog images of Agfa, Ilford, Kodak and Polaroid factories as they were abandoned, stripped and reduced to rubble. Burley's book thereby provides a useful example of thinking historically wrapped within what at first glance seems to be a romantic, or even Romanticist exercise i.e.

14. Burley, R. (2013).

the painstaking and potentially emotive documentation of new ruins. His book is a valedictory beatification of what is nevertheless exposed, in and by its destruction, to have been an ugly, polluting industry, involving corrosive chemical concoctions pervading darkened factory spaces.

Burley's accompanying text meanwhile provides statistics detailing the scale and pervasiveness of the chemical photography industry in its heyday, numbers that might still astound us, even in our own amazing and unprecedented age of exponentially escalating Big Data.

E.g. "At its peak in the 1980s, Kodak employed more than 60,000 people in Rochester New York, more than a quarter of the city's population at the time".[15]

Or: "Enschede, a town of 150,000... was home to Polaroid's European manufacturing facility... Established in 1865, the plant employed 1,200 workers and produced 1.5 billion packages (about 35 million per year) of Polaroid integral and peel–apart films before it was closed in 2008". [16]

Burley's research has more than one historical purpose and method. It may be elegiac, and faintly melancholic but he also takes trouble to historicise his object by relativising the phenomenon of our current digital media empires in comparison with their recently departed chemical equivalents. Possibly the most acidic point in the book comes when Burley concludes an introductory

15. Burley, R. (2013).
16. Burley, R. (2013).

essay with these words:

"The future, however, is unknown, and anachronisms cut both ways… Technologies are made to be transformed, and redefined, even reinvented. If this book is a eulogy… it is also an article of faith that anything is possible…"[17]

We might interpret this as a defiant statement, one of refusal and denial, like that of someone in the early stages of grief. However, there is also something laced into Burley's words which insists that we never know in which way history will flex, and, given this, one (possibly vengeful) implication might be that, just as Agfa, Ilford, Kodak and Polaroid, at the height of their success, could not have foreseen — as a result of rapid technological and market change — the sudden decline of their chemical industry, nor can today's digital empires (and all who enjoy their provision) imagine technological changes that will, in their turn, inevitably displace their pervasive, innovative technologies and render those too, unprofitable, unpopular and obsolete. Burley thus reminds us that thinking historically is always a refusal of any sense of complacency concerning the persistence and endurance of forms, values and technologies that we currently revere as new and which appear indispensable, in the way they seem to define and underpin our lives and even our reality.

17.   Burley, R. (2013).

ROMANCE AND ROMANTICISM

Pains are taken and lengths gone to in order to ensure that we see technology as novel and machines as fun. Technology's otherwise barbaric intervention may be dressed–up or assuaged with elements of design, ingratiating it to its audience, taking the edge off its shock. Some trace of this legacy is discernible within the Victoriana and quasi–orientalist designs pervading vintage carousels and other fairground rides. We might even say that the travelling fair has served and continues to serves as an allegorical interface between technological industrialisation and a more romantic aspect of our humanity.

Authentic, well–maintained vintage carousels come replete with a musical organ secreted at their heart, wheezing out once popular tunes while carved or moulded horses emulate gliding motions and circle their central hub. Everything is lavishly painted, often with patterns featuring arabesques so that the whole evokes a nomadic fantasy while subtly recalling the more natural, equine technology that industrial age machines and combustion engines (with their 'horsepower') rapidly and comprehensively displaced. Meanwhile, a fun fair's peripatetic, itinerant culture and easy flowing cash economy retains and perpetuates various traits of a nomadic culture, echoes of the gypsy, traveller, tinker and Roma.

Romance and Romanticism may be rooted in connections to the great, holy city of Rome and that city's historic empire, but Roma also refers to a people with no equivalent reputation for empire–building. The Roma of central Europe may have had a greater past, but if so it is currently obscured from popular perception by the passage of time.

Romance and Romanticism relate to travel, to nomadism, to art history and to narrative, as well as to a certain idiosyncratic and uncompromising persistence we might call heroic. Given their relevance to the Roma these terms might also come to implicate gleaning, craft, and subsistence economics, song, dance, poetics and freedom. Meanwhile, romance and Romanticism are crucially connected with books and stories.

Eighteenth and nineteenth century artists, writers and philosophers responded to the onset of modernity by thoroughly re–evaluating art's purpose, method, and the way it operates for and within society. Wordsworth and Coleridge had to provide a theoretical proviso, a manifesto–like preface for their innovative *Lyrical Ballads*.[1] Difficult as it is to believe today, they were afraid that their readers would not recognise or value their innovations *as* poems. Perhaps it is *here* that modernity's *avant–garde* is born, making the *avant–garde* consequently and inextricably Romantic.

The earliest modern artists may have tried to distinguish themselves from Romanticism as a sign of their own increasing modernity (Courbet, and in more complex ways Baudelaire too, strived to do so). Nevertheless, modern art perpetuates Romanticism by other means. Increasing familiarity with Walter Benjamin's writings on art, on artists, on history and modernity reveals his desire to

1.   Stafford, F. (2013).

maintain tradition *despite* modernity and to see modern art practices as ways and means of wresting or rescuing tradition from otherwise belligerent modern forces.

Recently, reading the Romantic poet John Clare's *The Gypsies' Evening Blaze*, I underwent a significant, uncanny, if at first unclear sense of recognition.[2] After reflecting on this I realised (in a kind of Sebald—ian revelation)[3] that this must have been the very poem that my English teacher, when I was just 12 years old, presented to the class and asked us to copy out for homework. I remember that (as if then, as a child, I had anticipated the present making of this very book) I responded with exceptional enthusiasm to this task, going beyond the call of duty and augmenting my rendition with an unsolicited illustration of the picture it conjured in my mind. I used thick crayons to exuberantly describe a flickering fire that illuminated, against a blackened sky, a curve of wagons of the kind I imagined gypsies might occupy.[4]

My teacher publicly celebrated my enthusiastic response and the outcome might be considered both the high and low point of my secondary education. She held my work up as an example to the whole class, while embarrassingly

---

2. Clare, J. (2007).

3. Sebald, W. G. (2001)., and Sebald, W. G. (2002). W.G. Sebald's innovative and celebrated contributions to history writing involve many perambulations, as well as plays with memory that include *satori*—like moments of revelation.

4. O'Kane, P. (2014). An admiring reference can be found within my previous **eeodo** publication *Where Is That Light Now?* to "the illustrations of Ardizzone" enjoyed during childhood reading. This, combined with the anecdote above, seems to reveal a previously un—noted but deep—rooted passion for illustrated narratives that I am fortunate enough to be still pursuing, here, in the mature stage of my life and career.

referring to me as the 'light of her life'. At the next play-time I found myself surrounded by boys baying 'FIGHT!' 'FIGHT!' and, looking around to see who was in trouble, experienced bewilderment, pain, humiliation and shame as a 'friend' knocked me over, pinned me down and repeatedly thumped me in the eye, to the delight of the chanting crowd.

Decades later, as I began to write this book, a therapist saw in this tale the stark juxtaposition of proud, personal triumph followed immediately by violent, public put–down. She thus suggested it might have played a significant part in my psychological, social and professional development. On further reflection it may well be true that academic experiences like this, so strongly contrasted with extra–curricular activities I enjoyed as a child in the woods and fields surrounding our housing estate (and then again as a teenager on its sulphur–lit night streets), led me to abandon school and take daily, truanting detours alone on paths and pavements, through woods and parks, occasionally conducting conversations with wayward cats and dogs for whom I developed an empathic bond stronger than any with my teachers or fellow pupils.

As a result, at sixteen, I left school, without friends, contacts or kudos; with no plans, power, direction or qualifications other than a single, grade B, 'O' Level Art — plus one modest prize, a historical novel awarded by the same English teacher at the end of that watershed year featuring the poem and the beating. If the Romantic model of the *Bildungsroman*[5] occasionally seems to influence this, and others of my writings, as they push and pull between aspirations to academicism and indulgence in memoir, the source of any such affectation may lie within the events just described.

The Romantic poet John Clare (1793–1864) may appear to offer a familiar and easy entrance to what we think of as Romanticism, however, continued scrutiny of our theme inevitably reveals its scale and complexity. Nevertheless, a good reason for pursuing Romanticism, even at this seemingly unlikely moment, might be to help understand where our modern world, modern art, modernism and modernity all stem from. Romanticism is commonly, chronologically, agreed to immediately precede modern art. As an ism it may not represent an epoch as a whole but rather certain cultural and aesthetic, philosophical and psychological ways and means, purportedly developed to comprehend, withstand and negotiate an epoch fundamentally determined, to an unprecedented degree, by new technological factors.

Clare repeatedly noted in his relatively simple, descriptive poems of rural life (which stand in contrast to the more canonically conscious, academically informed works of more 'elevated' Romantics) the encroaching influence of modernity and capitalism, e.g. in the enclosure of what was previously common land. In more than one poem

---

5. *Bildungsroman* is the literary term for a Romanticist novel of formation, a coming–of–age story, focusing on psychological and moral growth from youth to adulthood. *Bildungsroman* is strongly associated with publication of *Wilhelm Meister's Apprenticeship* by Johann Wolfgang Goethe, in 1795–6.

Clare appears to have envied the people he refers to as "gypsies" their special mode of existence, nomadism, proximity to nature and adherence to tradition. This gypsy lifestyle seemed then, and still perhaps seems now, to be the antithesis of a dynamic and aspirational capitalism that hijacks, diverts and exacerbates our traditions, needs, economies and desires, shackling us to more or less alienated labour, wedding us to mortgaged bricks and mortar, to the '9 to 5' and the commuter's working week, leaving perhaps only the Sunday drive or Sunday walk — a relatively non–instrumentalised, purely recreational journey — to perpetuate any trace of a lost, more nomadic and romantic culture.

Perhaps the gypsy represented for Clare,[6] and might again for us today, not only a lost past, or abandoned alternative but also a possible future, an exemplary model for a society riven, rinsed, and we might say 'ruined', by sedentary, centralised urbanism, and by modern, capitalist economics.

But rather than hastily press Clare into the service of current political debate, here are a few extracts[7] from his poems to serve us as illustrations, or even to provide a brief interlude:

6. Morrison, V. (1970)., and Morrison, V. (1979). Songwriter Van Morrison also invoked the gipsy, the mystic, and chivalry in his classic, early 1970s period of songwriting.

7. Clare, J. (2007). All the following citations are based on the Faber & Faber edition *John Clare: poems selected by Paul Farley.*

Trespass by John Clare

I dreaded walking where there was no path
And pressed with cautious tread the meadow swath
And always turned to look with wary eye
And always feared the owner coming by;
Yet everything about where I had gone
Appeared so beautiful I ventured on
And when I gained the road where all are free
I fancied every stranger frowned at me
And every kinder look appeared to say
'You've been on trespass in your walk today'.
I've often thought, the day appeared so fine,
How beautiful if such a place were mine;
But, having naught, I never feel alone
And cannot use another's as my own.

From *Remembrances* by John Clare

By Langley Bush I roam, but the bush hath left its hill;
On Cowper Green I stray, 'tis a desert strange and chill;
And spreading Lea Close Oak, ere decay had penned its will,
To the axe of the spoiler and self–interest fell a prey;
And Crossberry Way and old Round Oak's narrow lane
With its hollow trees like pulpits, I shall never see again;
Enclosure like a Bonaparte let not a thing remain,
It levelled every bush and tree and levelled every hill
And hung the moles for traitors – though the brook is
     running still,
It runs a naked stream, cold and chill.

From *The Fallen Elm* by John Clare

It grows the licence of o'erbearing fools
To cheat plain honesty by force of might.
Thus came enclosure — ruin was its guide
But freedom's clapping hands enjoyed the sight
Though comfort's cottage soon was thrust aside
And workhouse prisons raised upon the site.
E'en nature's dwellings far away from men —
The common heath — become the spoiler's prey:
The rabbit had not where to make his den
And labour's only cow was drove away.
No matter — wrong was right and right was wrong
And freedom's bawl was sanction to the song.

From *The Lament of Swordy Nell* by John Clare

There was a time my bit of ground
Made freemen of the slave;
The ass no pindar'd dare to pound
When I his supper gave;
The gypsies' camp was not afraid,
I made his dwelling free,
Till vile enclosure came and made
A parish slave of me.

The gypsies further on sojourn,
No parish bounds they like . . .

From *The Gipsy Camp* by John Clare

'Tis thus they live — a picture to the place,
a quiet, pilfering, unprotected race.

The Gypsies' Evening Blaze by John Clare

To me how wildly pleasing is that scene
Which doth present in evening's dusky hour
A group of gypsies centred on the green
In some warm nook where Boreas has no power,
Where sudden starts the quivering blaze behind
Short shrubby bushes nibbled by the sheep
That mostly on these shortsward pastures keep,
Now lost, now seen, now bending with the wind:
And now the swarthy sybil kneels reclined,
With proggling stick she still renews the blaze,
Forcing bright sparks to twinkle from the flaze.
When this I view, the all–attentive mind
Will oft exclaim (so strong the scene pervades)
'Grant me this life, thou spirit of the shades!'

Reflecting on these connections now, I see that some form of Romanticism was laid down in me as a child, as if for future use or survival, by a father who must have greatly missed the countryside of his Irish homeland and childhood. He grafted away in England as a dutiful commuter, patiently scaling the lower rungs of the civil service, rapidly burning up (he died sadly young) his limited energy, while stretching a thin income across a family of seven crammed into a four–bedroom council house.

By way of compensation for all this restriction, my parents afforded us exceptional freedom to experiment wildly and organically with our youthful creativity. Bedroom walls were plastered with a collage of images, and our proto–bands, with drums and amps, rehearsed inside the house. But at an earlier age mum and dad had also indoctrinated us into nature of another kind, during regular weekend walks into the flat farmland surrounding our estate. There we learned the names of every tree, identifiable by their fruits, the shapes of their leaves, and their overall profile. We knew species of birds by their song, size and flight, and learned to hush, point, and marvel at the hover of a Kestrel, the aerobatics of a Swift or the melodies of an unseen Thrush. Then, trundling home on nettle–stung legs, we might nod, a little less enthusiastically now, in response to the languid flap of a Peewit, making its way across the sunset.

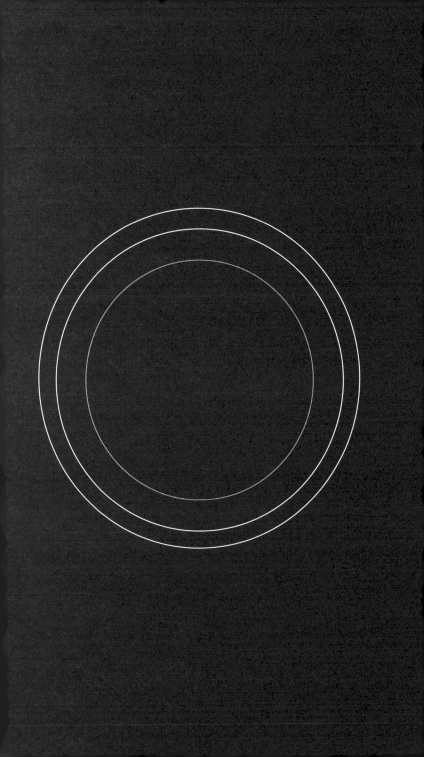

ROMANCING
THE CITY

A Modern Art history course will often begin in Paris, with Manet's 1860s provocations or Baudelaire's spirited 1840s call for an art appropriate to his own epoch. However, as soon as we mention Baudelaire's name we realise that, to understand modern art we need to know something of Romanticism, if only to comprehend the way in which modern art refuted, contrasted with, or grew out of Romanticism. Was modern art a challenge to, an alternative to, or (less dramatically, but just as significantly) an *extension* and proliferation of Romanticism by other means?

A modern state of mind, a modern approach to time and history may be informed by modernity as an exceptional cultural phenomenon, though arising, not out of nowhere but rather out of historical contiguity, connections and contingencies. While Baudelaire's *Salon of 1846*[1] appears to call for a modern Realism, his modern poetry, and much of his writing on painting were still infused with elements of Romanticism and traces of Symbolism. He transmitted an enthusiasm for intoxication, colour and passion that went beyond the more modern, austere and realist contents and modes called for in *Of The Heroism of Modern Life* (1846).[2] Thus we see Baudelaire as someone struggling with cultural change, striving to rescue direction, meaning and value, and even to save tradition from a potentially bleak scenario, and thus to rescue art, culture and poetry, for himself, his fellow artists, and for an emerging, innately revolutionary modern society.

1. Baudelaire, C. (1992). pp. 47–107.
2. Baudelaire, C. (1992). pp. 104–107.

Today, we may all be Baudelaires, never complacent concerning tradition nor comfortable with our current ism, but tasked to occupy, negotiate and construct our own times, while attempting to orientate ourselves by means of poetic, rhetorical and hyperbolic postures, gestures and hypotheses. We might feel sufficiently, and justifiably heroic in simply withstanding the present as we clumsily stumble into an unprepossessing future, barely guided by shifting images of a much disputed past.

Baudelaire recognised the unprecedented influences imposed upon poetry, on artists in general, and on our humanity by the technology of Paris as the first modern city. He also noted the value of a certain kind of information supplied by newspapers and the way in which the importance of news might supplant or become synthesised with established, traditional, Classical, and Neoclassical narratives of the epic and heroic.[3] When Baudelaire called for a heroism of modern life he was redirecting Romanticism and allowing tradition to persist in modern garb.

We may live lives that seem humdrum in comparison with knights of medieval legend, biblical characters or Homer's protagonists, but Baudelaire suggests we must and do have a heroism of our own, one that we must always search for and recognise within our modern selves and changing environment. This neo–Romantic quest is perpetual and perennial, concerned not just with connecting the distant past to a progressive narrative but in thereby updating tradition to enable it to survive modernity.

---

3. Consider James Joyce's *Ulysses* (1922). Or T.S. Eliot's *The Waste Land* (1922).

Thus the *flâneur* of Baudelaire's *milieu* is eventually inherited by Charlie Chaplin's tramp perambulating across our cinema screen. Meanwhile we might look back from Baudelaire's perspective to find precedents and models in Don Quixote's exceptional adventuring, or Scheherazade's[4] narrative nomadism.[5] Nihilistic 1970s punks, or alienated 80s *otaku*[6] also appear as extensions of a tradition that embodies hero and anti–hero but which always throws up a necessary guide to a challenging time, invariably defined by technological progress.

Some of Walter Benjamin's earliest major writings aimed to rearticulate the dynamic relationship between modernity and Romanticism, and this project continued to occupy him, using various approaches and experiments, throughout his life and career.[7] So while we might discern in Benjamin's work certain tensions between iconoclastic, nothing–if–not–modern Marxism, and ancient Jewish faith's deep immersion in tradition, Benjamin's complex, sometimes mysterious, but never quite mystical approach to time, history, futurity, and redemption can also be seen to derive from his formative interest in Romanticism, a cultural and historical arena within which the ancient and modern enjoy a profound and productive encounter.

Benjamin translated his experience into inspired and

---

4. Lyons, M. C. (Trans.). (2008).
5. Cervantes, M. de. (1950).
6. *Otaku*, originally used to describe technologically isolated and obsessive, geeky 1980s Tokyo teenagers.
7. Hanssen, B. & Benjamin, A. (Eds.). (2002).

enduring observations that can now be endlessly scrutinised and re–evaluated as the least dogmatic of truths.
His fascination with fragments, moments, ruins, constellations and monads enable ways of articulating the
presence of the universal in the particular, the whole
in the part, and the past in the present, all as a means of
attempting to divine possible futures. Benjamin's sense
of responsibility to the future appears to be informed by
belief in an untimely wisdom that overspills the bounds
of merely reasonable, rational, modern or academic
knowledge. He prefers storytelling to information and
his thought arises from an un–prejudicial synthesis of
Romanticism, Marxism and Jewish culture — arguably
the three major epistemes with which he experimented
in search of his own method of evaluating experience and
representing modernity in as holistic and *thereby* accurate
a manner as possible.

Inspired by Benjamin we might wish to draw our study
further back in time and in history, from Benjamin's Europe to Baudelaire's Paris, then on and back perhaps to
the Jena of Novalis and consequently the considerations
of Schlegel, Fichte, Hölderlin and Goethe, questioning
how Romanticism might have emerged as a response to,
or extension of Kant's thought, and also how Benjamin's
methods, along with the critical theory of his Frankfurt
School associates, might have differed from, and yet also
perpetuated a post–Kantian Romanticist project by other
means?

Both Benjamin and Baudelaire applied the solvent of imaginative interpretation to the experience of the modern

city, to loosen (by articulating) the bonds of a phenomenon within which we might feel justifiably incarcerated.
We earlier noted a perambulatory model informing John
Clare's poetry, and all Romantics tend to travel, move, go
on lone, roving journeys, discovering, achieving or merely
surviving as a constant, cultural refugee by means of motion, as do Roma, Gypsies, Bedouins and Knights.

A Romantic, perambulatory spirit is clearly discerned
in the model of the *flâneur,* that exception to the urban
rule who may incorporate chivalric and Quixotic traces
of a Romanticism otherwise seemingly diminished by
modernity. The *flâneur's* object needs to be rescued and
redeemed according to a noble quest, but rather than a
damsel or grail, that object becomes a redemptive, poetic
observation, perhaps an ironic reflection on the times.
Meanwhile, what needs to be pursued, rescued, preserved
and maintained, through and despite modernity (while
never shielded from modernity), is tradition, which incorporates no less than our most precious, honed and
valued human traits.

Despite the adamantine brutality of the city, romance
seeps in, bursts its tarmac, hangs from its bridges and loos-
ens its stones. Like ubiquitous Buddleia lilacs erupting
from flaws in a barren façade to grow into epic creatures,
so modern poetry, and modern poetic thought — never
wholly distinguishable from the Romantic tradition
— might arise irrepressibly, at any place or time within
the city's apparently inauspicious labyrinth. Similarly,
modern anti–heroes, from Baudelaire and Benjamin, on
through to punk and post–punk poets — the doomy Ian

Curtis, the manic John Lydon or John Cooper Clarke, the character of 'Johnny' in Mike Leigh's (1993) film *Naked* — all embody something of the inventive and evasive spirit of Scheherazade as well as the folly of *Don Quixote as they* pursue their respective quests in comet–like outbursts, playful pratfalls or intricately woven trajectories through a shifting culture of modern taste and ideas ever augmented by new twists, layers, challenges and tasks.[8] They necessarily venture beyond all comfort zones in search of some fragment of elusive, barely recognisable glory.

Baudelaire and Benjamin, both branded by historical responsibility, insisted that despite their enthusiasm for embracing and articulating modernity within the new environment of the modern city, a Romantic spirit remains an intrinsic element of their calling and must therefore be nourished. It falls to the poet, the dandy, the *flâneur* and critical theorist to perform the civic duty of daily scoping and sweeping the streets, rejuvenating their surface with imaginative observation and divine interpretation, thus keeping a way (the possibility of living, with nobility and dignity, in and despite modernity) open, and keeping the way romantic (poetic, imaginative, individuated, adventurous) against all odds.

Benjamin gave the title *One Way Street* to one of the most resolved works he published in his lifetime.[9] While he romantically dedicated the book to, and associated its title

---

8. Leigh, M. (Director). (1993). The journey of Mike Leigh's 'Johnny' in his film *Naked* might be compared with that of Orpheus through the underworld.

9. Benjamin, W. (2000).

with, love and his lover, Asja Lacis, the original cover, de-signed by Sasha Stone, interprets the title by emphasising modernity and the modern city as the particular, secular-ised, perhaps dangerously singular and narrow way that we have chosen by which to progress. Benjamin's later *Theses on a Philosophy of History*[10] also challenges and even satirises habitual images and models of time and history as all–too–directional, singular and linear.

The city may be a technology, and yet the city is undenia-bly romantic. Modernity ages all too soon, the outmoded appearing as its constant corollary, the inevitable, yet unanticipated, companion of the new. The city betrays traces of the past and even memories of the rural, while arrogantly presuming that its exceptional modernity tri-umphs over both. The city limit is where a compensatory, escapist, rural Romanticism ends and a gnarled, anxious, *synthetic* Romanticism is wrested and wrangled from the built environment. This *synthetic* Romanticism marks the modernising achievement of Baudelaire, of contempo-raries like Poe, and of early modern art.[11]

The city may be soaked through with technologies, then as now construction sites attesting to sinuous sewers and roots that up–thrusting walls and gleaming foyers will eventually belie, and yet the canyons created by modern

---

10. Benjamin, W. (1968). pp. 253–264.

11. Benjamin, W. (1973)., and Benjamin, W. (1985). Noting both Poe's and Baude-laire's and other Parisian contemporaries' romantic allusions to Native American Indians as comparable with modern city dwellers. Benjamin refers to these in *Charles Baudelaire, A Lyric Poet in the Era of High Capitalism*, but also remarks on the trend for a certain 'romantic' Apache trope prevalent in the theatre visits documented in *Moscow Diary*.

architecture produce a strange terrain in which a lone, emotive subject, cast into cold uncertainty by the strain placed on threatened tradition, might wander, free at least to wonder,[12] as might a painter or poet of an earlier age and within a more natural wilderness.[13]

The city rises, rumbles, away, beneath and over, breaking its own bounds, mocking the gates that once marked its limits, leaving us awed, thrilled and yet still servicing the megalopolis like minions who increasingly regard access to its heart to be a privilege. Come snowstorm, terror alert, labour strike or simply Sunday, the city can nevertheless reveal itself, not only as a grinding machine but also as a calm, desert–like terrain, through and over which we pass with renewed trepidation. While on a stormy night, some rare, commercially or municipally nurtured tree, persisting within the city's precious bounds, might yet lash its windswept mane against a glowing glass façade, allowing a brief outburst of suffering to meld in a flash with the sombre joy of sublime experience.[14]

---

12. Sebald, W. G. (2001). Here, it is impossible not to think of the nocturnal and urban perambulations informing W.G. Sebald's *Austerlitz*.

13. The 'gumshoe' of *film noir* fame can easily be seen as a legacy of Romanticism here. It also maps on to Benjamin's famous reference to the comparison of Atget's photographic rendering of Parisian views with 'scenes of a crime'.

14. Some recent paintings by Alex Katz communicate this sense of a contemporary sublime persisting as if within and despite a simulacral twenty first century bourgeois lifestyle.

CANDLE TIME

A certain Parisian lamppost, painted by Van Gogh in 1886 and subsequently celebrated by the influential social art historian T. J. Clark, once signified the border between country and city and thus between future and past, tradition and modernity, and implicitly between Romanticism and modern art. It stood in what might be fashionably referred to today as a liminal zone or non–place, where the unnatural, technological spectacle of the city's illuminated nights (memorably rendered by Camille Pissaro) might begin, and where the countryside was left behind, along with a pre–industrial past in which only candles and God might get the living through the night.[1]

Today, candles have accumulated semiotic cultural value as a technology regularly deployed in scenarios wherein it is deemed appropriate to construct a certain 'romantic' and nostalgic atmosphere. Candles (along with their battery–operated equivalents, torches, LED lights, smartphones etc.)[2] may also come into play in the event of that most modern of afflictions, the power–cut, a traumatic occasion which transports us suddenly to the

---

1. Clark, T. J. (2003). p. 25. (*The Outskirts of Paris* by Vincent Van Gogh, 1886). The history of the landscape and the suburbs (or *environs*), in art and in culture, could also be pursued here with reference to the *Campagna* in the history of European painting.

2. Protests in twenty first Century Korea seem to have preserved something of the romantic spirit at the heart and the origin of modern revolution. In recent mass vigils participants identified themselves by carrying candles, adapted to the wind and to the hand by the artful use of a paper cup. One government minister, affronted by the protests, claimed they would quickly fade away and purposefully deployed the metaphor of candles melting away or easily blown out by the wind. However, the protests have only persisted and grown, further enabled by the availability of battery operated, imitation candles and an exuberant plethora of LED equivalents.

'foreign country' of the past,[3] where we quickly discover that, denied electricity, we lack many fundamental tools, technologies and services on which we depend for every-day comforts and even our survival. Given this temporary deficit we are briefly thrown back into history, forced to rediscover the idiosyncratic values and charms of prior technologies that have been unceremoniously side–lined on the rapid march through and to modernity, novelty and progress.

A candle might still be cherished and valued today for the anachronistic way in which it illuminates a room with a special *in*constancy, less steadily, less powerfully than the gas and electric illuminations that followed and supplanted it in historical procession, and which have become increasingly emphatic symbols of modernity itself.[4] Meanwhile the candle provides us with a relatively simple technological representation of passing time, to which the electric bulb only alludes when it silently, in-visibly, fails or pops–off, and when we rummage for or purchase a replacement.

Despite its status as a symbol of a rational, scientific age, purged of gloom, shadows, ignorance and superstition (the light bulb even came to signify an idea), there is still a

---

3. "The past is a foreign country; they do things differently there". The often quoted first line of L.P. Hartley's 1953 novel *The Go–Between*.

4. Consider the 'white cube' style art gallery space, which, as if to proclaim its ultra — or exemplary modernity, seems ever–more intensely illuminated, to the point where we might tentatively predict that it will one day blind us to the values and qualities of any art placed within it, unless of course, that art is specifically designed to keep–up with the exponentially increasing brilliance of its changing context.

lingering element of *vanitas* about the modern light bulb, something vaguely fatal, morbid and ghostly about its milky, sealed and gaseous interior that perhaps reminds us of our own fragile form and ultimate, breathless end.[5] Furthermore, there is something about its unexpected, explosive failure, just at the moment when we habitually summon its convenience, that is capable of exposing an ancient yet repressed sense of fate and foreboding in even the most rational modern subject, as if the whole of our modernity had failed us in a flash.

If it is excusable to switch again here into subjective, memoir mode, I recall that, during an ill–fated and all–too–soon abandoned arts degree in Photography, Film & Television, I once observed a technician pains-takingly setting up a video camera in a crepuscular TV studio, apparently to record, or perhaps broadcast (as passively and fixedly as any CCTV system) a single, light-ed candle burning down. I do not know the technician's name, whether he was also an artist and this a work of art or simply a test or demonstration arranged for the in-struction of students, but I was aware, without enquiring, that the arrangement suggested a meaningful, even phil-osophical interplay of two disparate and anachronistic technologies by means of which a certain period of time would be represented in a thought–provoking manner.

This contrived arrangement proffered a hybrid, or synthe-sis of what might be called 'candle time', 'video time' and

---

5. Fei, C. (Artist). (2006). *Whose Utopia?* A short film by artist Cao Fei, movingly articulates both the tiresome routines and possible dreams of workers in an Osram light bulb factory in China.

'real time', each being co–present as if to test the other's validity or accuracy, and to enquire which was the correct or
optimum way to visualise, experience, measure or record
passing time? Juxtaposing the two technologies, one ancient and romantic, the other (at the time) the cutting edge
of modern technology, not only compared their relative
simplicity and complexity but invoked relativism itself,
moving the viewer to suspect that time can*not* be accurately or objectively represented but is always determined
according to a particular perception while manifest and
measured by means of a particular image or materialisa-
tion. Meanwhile, what we often lazily objectify simply as
'time' may or may not be other to whichever technology
we choose to measure and represent it.

Years later I saw a well–known work by the painter Ger-
hard Richter, depicting little more than a candle, painted,
as Richter often paints, with conscious reference to the
mediating technology of photography, and thus rendered
in a way that draws into play the artist's comprehensive
exploration of the manifold ways in which time might be
represented by an oil painter in an age of photography
(also of cinema, video, digital and atomic clocks, and
candles too). By making oil paintings of photographs of
candles Richter draws us into a *mise–en–abyme* involving
a layered history and implicating several technologies of
romance.

Richter's passion for photography is only one aspect
of a multi–faceted painting practice that also includes
carefully paced scrapes, drags and wipes of paint which
materially and demonstrably embody and record time

in the particular form of a linear passage. However, in another well–known Richter painting, *Betty* (1988), we see the back of his daughter's head, again painted from and through the mediating technology of a photograph. The girl's turning away is familiar as a gesture found in many Romanticist scenes wherein a lone figure might gesturally demonstrate their own, ultimate (we might say fatally) subjective isolation. In turning away from us a figure appears to turn in on itself, even as, in turning, it may also turn towards others or on to a world beyond our own perceptions and concerns. We are nevertheless denied, if not shunned and rendered alone.[6]

This enigmatic gesture might then remind us of our own ultimate solitude, if not in life generally then at least as viewers of art as we come to Richter's painting prepared to make that special, subjective, yet also strangely objective ('Alone, But Not Lonely')[7] aesthetic judgement which tested Kant's reasonable schema with an apparent paradox.[8] The special and strange echo of our self (our own looking, our own alone–ness) that we sense in the image of an averted face, might again draw us into a *mise–en–abyme* wherein we can expect to discover little more than some inevitable pathos, illustrating our ultimate alone–ness or loneliness as an individually embodied soul.

---

6. Here we might tease out a subtle link or unexpected connection to the so–called 'attention economy' as it embroils and employs today's youth in particular, while implicating everyone using computers, particularly online.

7. Grassmuck, V. (2016). Reference to the 1990 essay *"I'm Alone, But Not Lonely"* by Volker Grassmuck. An edited version was produced as a 2016 book published by **eeodo**.

8. Kant, I. (1987)., and Caygill, H. (1995).

Meanwhile, being alone is strongly associated with romance and Romanticism. Perhaps the most famous line of English Romantic poetry compares human loneliness with the condition of a cloud, an image that has also become synonymous with collective, online, virtual communications. The meteorological cloud, the electronic cloud, and the lone (actual or virtual) subject can all be seen as untethered, undirected, free to roam or go wherever whim or winds may blow.

For the Romantics, lone experience, a dialogue between self and unknown, created a heroic and historic sense of constantly verging on discovery. Novelty is out there, waiting to be rescued from invisibility by an inspired vision. Some such Romanticism, in some measure, surely resides in us, latent even in the most cynical, ironic, downtrodden, over–technologised or otherwise eviscerated lives.

It seems therefore justifiable to appeal to a universal propensity to redeem the self by means of narrative; to rescue the 'damsel' of the self by means of a certain romance; and to rescue romance itself as a precious value hidden at the heart even of the most modern life and its potential for meaningful narrative. This singularly savoured subjectivity is, after all, a most affordable means of survival, available to convicts and kings and capable of clarifying our fundamental sense of purpose, despite the disinterestedness of others; despite life's unavoidable ordure and onerous ordeals; despite the unacceptably unjust incompatibility of each life with its death; despite all, our internal narrative is something we must love and cherish, protecting the story of our life, our life as story, and *thus* as meaningful.

Nevertheless, the unarguable popularity of our current techno–individualism has surprised us. *Cafés* and canteens, once hives of gossip, chat and banter, and even breeding places of dissent and revolution, now target and cater for those who prefer to eat silently and alone with their device. Any eyeline that might bring an individuated, *latté*–sipping screen–scroller into unmediated contact with another human being, can be artfully negated by designers of dining facilities who may also position single chairs and tiny tables up against windows and walls.

Given the opportunity (or perhaps having had it insidiously imposed upon us) millions of closet romantics have emerged into visibility. Being indirectly and virtually connected to the crowd or cloud, yet immediately and actually isolated ('Alone, But Not Lonely') has proven preferable, possibly because of the control it awards us over our schedules and relationships, just one aspect of the new freedoms awarded us by new technologies. However, in this process we surely technologise and instrumentalise our lives and relationships to an unprecedented degree. The twenty first century meaning of Friends, Likes and *emojis* all attest to the technologisation of aspects of human life and relationships once cherished as a less utilitarian preserve.

Politically then, we might fear the worst, if that is, we assume our newly hushed, disjointed and distracted crowd is any less critically engaged than those "absent–minded" 1930s cinema–goers in whom Benjamin appeared to invest political faith,[9] but who were nevertheless corralled by ideologies that successfully utilised contemporary technologies to lead their society to its physical and moral destruction.

9. Benjamin, W. (1968). pp. 217–251. *The Work of Art in the Age of Mechanical Reproduction*, Section XV. p. 241.

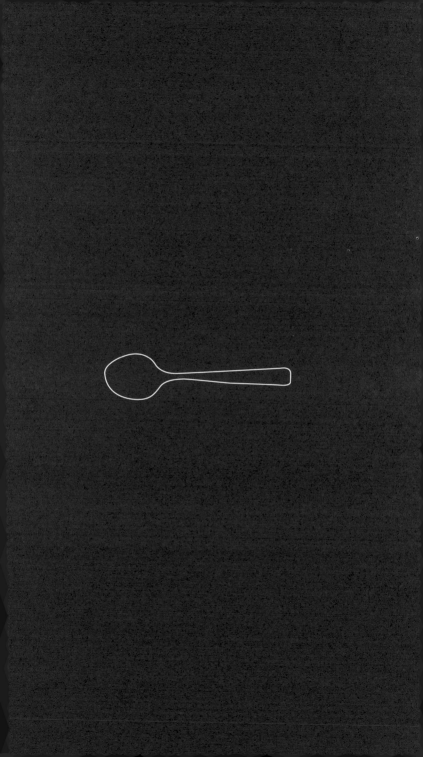

LIFE, DEATH, LOVE & NARRATIVE

Romance heightens the quality of our perceived journey through, in, with, and *as* time. Romance is a certain being *in* time, a being *steeped in* time we might say, as Proust's tea was steeped in hot water and his madeleine steeped in tea. Even if, in romantic love we lose track of time, are consumed by or lost in time; even if time, in love, expands like an accordion, ridiculing any more parsimonious sense of temporal duty, romance is always a being in time, perhaps its richest example, summoning us to serve adventure not utility, even to gamble our very lives, as we enter a realm of risk, for better or worse.

Romance is never an objective understanding of, or mathematically measurable relationship with time, but rather a duration, an experiential and emotional embodiment of narrative experience that is necessarily subjective, unprecedented, untranslatable and seemingly unlike the experience of any possible other. Romance is thus always an embodied solitude, even when that solitude grows into the intractable unity of lovers, dissolving in the secret of a shared and singular love.[1] There and then time is no longer perceived in terms of a coherent or constructive narrative but rather as something material, formless and immanent.

And yet time's inexorable mobility will make of every life a drama, tragedy, epic or romance. Whether for the wealthy or the lowly, the aged or for those whose life

---

1.   Duras, M. (2006)., Duras, M. (1986)., Fletcher, J. & Calder, J. (Eds.) (1986)., and Robbe–Grillet, A. (1965). Marguerite Duras and Alain Robbe–Grillet demonstrated this admirably in the literary experiments that became known as *Nouveau Roman*. See also: Fletcher, J. & Calder, J. (Eds.). (1986).

lasts only days or moments, *every* life is determined by its *denouement* when the touch of death gives otherwise ungraspable existence a degree of final form.

Romance is a constant and honourable acknowledgement of the formidable force of our inevitable mortality. To live a life as a story is always to be conscious of its end, an end thus manifest, latent, in every material and eventful moment.

It thus seems hard to deny a certain literary quality influencing the way we understand and give a meaning to bare existence, thereby dressing it morally, purposefully, and nobly as *persistence*, investing bare life with the tenacity of a journey, a challenge, a tale from which — despite all choice and will — we are unable to escape and to which there is, after all, no alternative. Lives are innately heroic.

Charles Baudelaire called for a modern equivalent of Classical heroism, and in doing so alluded to the inextricable relationship between heroism and every life — long, short, grand or abject, ancient or modern.

On Kawara (1932–2014), the Japanese born painter and conceptual artist, with whose apparently minimal aesthetic we might hesitate to associate romance or Romanticism, nevertheless provides a useful contribution here due to the various ways in which he recorded apparently banal and uneventful daily existence as a conscious *persistence*.

Meanwhile, the Romantic philosopher Nietzsche warned,

not only of the implications of the death of God but of the enduring vitality of the "god of grammar".[2] In doing so he made us more vigilantly aware, not only of the laws of syntax ruling our language, psychology and perceptions, but of the omnipotence of grammar *as* narrative and narrative as grammar, and thus of the ultimate unavoidability of our inevitable, innate, ancient and enduring Romanticism.

A life and its story may be interpreted and made meaningful as a romance, but a story of any kind is also a technology, a machine, or contrivance. The book too is a particular technology, with its own history. However, the stories it may contain and the language used to impart those stories may also be described as technologies. They are contraptions, prostheses, devices or tools by means of which a certain task or duty is performed and something useful is transmitted. In his essay *The Storyteller* Walter Benjamin unpacked the distinction between the (ancient) story, the (Romantic or modern) novel, and (yet more modern) information.[3] Benjamin seemed to lament, to some extent, the loss of the story's power and pervasiveness in modern life along with the (ancient) storyteller's art and the loss of opportunities and motivations for amassing, sharing and telling stories afforded by the particular itinerant lifestyles and artisanal occupations that once fuelled both the art of storytelling and stories themselves.

2. Nietzsche, F. (1990). *'Reason' in Philosophy*, Section V.
3. Benjamin, W. (1968). pp. 83–109., and Benjamin, W. (2016).

The novel, first as something self–consciously written as a book by a lone author, then furnished into the object of a book, designed for the hand and thus anticipating reception by a lone reader in the private act of silent reading, is an altogether different cultural phenomenon (Benjamin points out) to the origins and tradition of the story and its collective telling. If the novel has, in some respects, usurped the purpose and position of the story, then information, in its turn, does something similar to the novel.

Benjamin discusses journalism as an example of information, a kind of technologised, verified, modern, short–lived and immediate echo or remnant of the traditional story. He also hints at statistics (mentioned elsewhere in his writings as possible harbingers or associates of fascism) and facts, which are traditionally much sought after, disputed, and used to justify the quality and status of modern journalism.

However, stats, facts and information, Benjamin suggests, have none of the compelling mystique and ultimately profound and enduring meaning of stories, which, in their very unreliability and inconsistency (they are passed on verbally, aurally, fragmentarily and as memories) nevertheless take on a special status and authority in the act of their live rendition, often by tellers who have returned from places of which we know little or nothing.

Some of the best–selling novels in Japan during the past ten or twenty years have been thumbed (rather than typed) on cell phones,[4] and there is no doubt that, even in a society like that of hypermodern Japan — also said to be having less sex, less human romance, but more technological romance[5] — the ability to communicate across distances, wherever we are in the world, and at whatever moment of the day or night, has, among other things, new kinds of romantic implications.

The narratives of our lives have been consistently extended, or in other ways transformed by technologies. It has even been claimed that the invention of the bicycle led to an increase in the average height of modern Europeans as the new technology enabled romantic liaisons and relationships between people of more distant communities (a love affair with a boy in the next village rather than the boy next door).[6]

While mobile phone use soon led to sexting it is equally true that the postal service, telephone, railway and bicycle were all technologies that, in their turn and in their time, changed the kinds of relationships and romances available to us, as well as transforming the twists and turns, shapes and possibilities of the narratives of those relationships and lives. Alfred Hitchcock, in his film *Dial M for Murder* (1954)[7] made his plot hinge on the possibilities

---

4. See e.g. *Deep Love* (2003) by a Tokyo man who simply calls himself Yoshi. Subsequently rendered as a multi–million selling book, plus multiple TV series' and a movie.

5. Holdsworth, J. (Director & Producer). (2013). Subject of a BBC documentary titled *No Sex Please We're Japanese*.

6. Possibly an urban myth but hard to resist including in a project with this title.

7. Hitchcock, A. (Director). (1954).

and limitations of what we now call a land line telephone, a bulky device tethered to a particular place in a particular building. A recently made (c. 2006) artist's video[8] depicts no more than a telephone answering machine on which the film's audience hears replayed a series of increasingly concerned messages apparently left by friends and family of the owner. The messages subtly accumulate evidence of a tragic narrative, communicating the social, economic, physical, mental and ultimately fatal downfall of the intended (but absent) recipient.

Why does a departing train in an old movie or historical novel have power to move us? A train is a dirty, grinding, hulk of machinery, despite the fact that Monet painted them objectively, steaming in streams of light at the Gare St Lazare; despite the fact that designers have managed to mitigate their overt technology and even ingratiate us to their modern apparatus.

Nevertheless, the departing train differs from the departing horse–drawn carriage, if only because, once powered–up and under way, guided by rigid tracks and perhaps an equally immutable timetable, the train is relatively unstoppable. Thus relatively powerless humans, divided by a train's departure, are unable to interrupt or interfere with its progress, and it is this inexorability that makes a departing train a narrative device that is potentially romantic.

---

8.   At the time of printing this book I had searched long but unfortunately in vain to re–identify this memorable artwork. Readers are invited to correspond if you know any more details of the work described.

In the image of a train that, in departing, significantly separates lovers or loved ones, the machine, its tracks, its power, motion and schedule, together take on a sublime, inexorable quality, not unlike the setting of the sun or the onset of rain, thus providing an example of the visible procession of time over which we are thus reminded we have little or no control. The departing train, in separating lovers, is both a banal machine and a more grandiose *deus ex machina*, significantly changing our narrative and usurping human agency, which is thus forced to defer to a power superior to our own in influencing those events which may significantly shape our lives.

Today of course, lovers separated by a departing train might ironically exchange live video streams, showing each other's perspective in real time, and thereby possibly mitigating any emotional impact. Today the poet or novelist might escape to the wilderness in search of profound isolation and inspiration but would feel reckless, dramatic or irresponsible to purposefully leave their smartphone behind, after all (as a pragmatic partner might advise) many problems or dangers might be more easily resolved with the use of this convenient device.

But why today write a poem or novel at all, why write or make a book, why strive to represent the world in a subjective or idiosyncratic mode, why yearn for contact or appeal for understanding, why defer, divert or transform our correspondence with others when we are all always present to one another, and have found, as a result, that we have surprisingly similar things to say? Today, narrative, and romance as a form of narrative, may well fear being supplanted by the ubiquity and pervasiveness of our continuously represented experience. Might this mean the end of the road for narrative? Even perhaps, the death of romance?

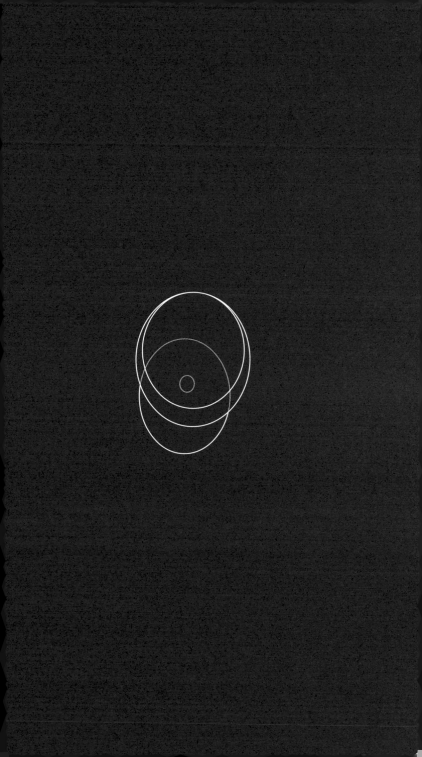

CANDY FLOSS
& DIESEL

Once or twice a year, a faceless piece of land in the centre of our estate nicknamed 'the wasteground', provided the community with a special kind of mechanised liberty.[1] The estate's builders and planners had thoroughly covered (with Roads, Avenues, Parades and Lanes, Drives and Greens, houses, flats maisonettes and shops, garages, parks, pubs and places of worship, schools, a Health Centre, a Community Centre, a Police Station and a Telephone Exchange) what must once have been acres of relatively flat farmland and woodland, wound around and through with a few country lanes and farmer's tracks.

Just beyond one end of the wasteground lay the estate's main shopping centre, while at the other lay several schools. Shoppers' minds might be burdened with weights and prices but children are nothing if not imaginative, particularly when progressing in the direction of school, and so the landscape of the wasteground may have been subtly imbued with a magical atmosphere imparted by the traces of a thousand tiny dreamers. Nevertheless, once or twice a year, a more mechanised type of magic would grace the wasteground in the form of a travelling fair.

The fair would arrive just before spring bank holiday, then come again in August, and perhaps in autumn too. It never arrived *en masse*, nor with any prior notice. Rather the event spread itself over the estate as a steadily

---

1.   During the avaricious 1980s the wasteground was built–over, rather rapidly, with a confusing warren of tiny, ungainly housing units, all–but defeating its purpose as any kind of thoroughfare, and consigning it to local cultural memory.

thickening rumour conveyed by a subcultural children's telegraph. One child would report to a small crowd that they had seen a car pulling a long caravan. Then a heavy trailer would be spied carrying a brightly coloured object visible through gaps in a tarpaulin. Adults took little interest in all of this but the children's network soon had the estate vibrating with anticipation until we would have to make a trip to the wasteground to confirm the rumours were true.

The wasteground would gradually fill with trucks, trailers and caravans, and for a while the rough land would continue to serve as an informal thoroughfare. But as established paths became increasingly churned–up or blocked, anyone intending to cross was forced to rethink their route, which also had to account for some tethered, mean–looking dogs. Our visitors relied on dry conditions, but whether the ground became sodden or remained firm they would always design new paths, using sawdust and wood chips, to lead us along a route that would ultimately prove most profitable for them.

Following a week of preparations, opening night would arrive. Again, details were gleaned through hearsay. This was a night to dress smarter if you could, and certainly to beg, steal or borrow cash for rides, games and slot machines. My very first romance occurred at the fair and turned out to be more pragmatic than passionate, more deceptive than true. It lasted precisely for the seven nights the fair was open and involved me paying for every one of my short–term girlfriend's rides, only for her to ditch me on the afternoon the fair closed down and left town.

Romance of a more reliable kind could nevertheless be gleaned from the fair's special mix of sensual amplitude, made available via a vibrant mix of technologies. At night, myriad coloured lightbulbs, each a relatively banal object in itself, together transformed the wasteground into a fantasy space, and whether you actively participated, or, your money spent, simply observed, you couldn't help being transported to another realm, albeit temporarily installed at the very heart of our humdrum estate.

While the fair rescued us from another bleak week of vacant evenings, its dramatic ephemerality made it a magical event. We knew this exception to our usual rule was fleeting, and made the most of it before the wasteground reverted to a nondescript thoroughfare servicing everyday necessities of shopping and school.

As well as flashing lights, bright colours, and eccentrically designed rides decorated with gaudy Victoriana and hints of orientalism, there was the all–important sound. The fair was a place where you could hear the latest soul, pop, funk and reggae hits (rock never quite seemed to fit) including banned records whose bawdy lyrics blasted defiantly into the night. While lights flashed in patterns and rides swung and flew, the music thumped and blared from huge speakers driven by powerful amplifiers.

This was altogether different to the relatively timid teen discos occasionally held at our Community Centre. Here there were young grown–ups, wide–eyed Romeos and time–tested teenage *fiancés* and *fiancées*, marauding gangs of guys and groups of gum–blowing girls. There were the estate's legendary beauties, style gurus, scrappers, would–be pop stars and dodgy dealers. All these celebrities would deftly negotiate the fair's mud and woodchip carpet, entering the sawdust–strewn arena in their best shoes, nodding, winking and waving to mates, while evil–eyeing enemies and rivals. Everyone played their necessary part in this proletarian pageant, stars for a night, for one week only, on stage together once or twice a year. Thus the dull and dormant estate, aroused by a fling with the fair and its itinerant troupe, would reveal an imaginative unconscious as we all immersed ourselves in this short–lived fantasy, the corollary of, and compensation for our ordinarily inauspicious, all too real way of life.

In addition to sights and sounds there were some special smells, and two in particular that memorably fused into one — candy floss and diesel. It is difficult to resist describing that pink substance, encountered (then at least) at no other time or place. Candy floss seemed to confirm that you had entered another world, where, as well as novel sights, sounds and disorientating motion, the staple diet was also exotic and bizarre. Just as adolescents know that as long as you dress fashionably you will never feel the cold, so they can also confirm that very little food is necessary to have a great time. Candy floss, an esoteric substance, supplied almost surreptitiously by the fair's mysterious merchants, seemed to prove this fact, it provided zero body–building nutrients and yet reeked of pure pleasure. Its almost virtual state was conjured out of air, accumulating around a narrow stick offered up to a gyrating machine. Once formed, and triumphantly grasped, you only had to flop it in the general direction of your face for its rose–coloured, viscose cloud to evaporate into you like saccharine perfume, providing you with no apparent benefit other than to briefly entertain — a procedure that might be considered a parody of consumption.

At the fair, suspended and inverted between earth and sky, then shot around in disorienting ellipses, all available time, money, energy and attention was dedicated to effortless pleasures. This was our little Las Vegas, and the only effort required was expended on the limp triggers of flimsy rifles aimed at dawdling ducks, or in casting misleading hoops over fishbowls (all the while fearful of winning a toy taller than yourself). We could also pump coins into a gaudily coloured, undulating mechanism whose arcane apparatus, piled high with previous punters' cash, kept us teetering on the slim chance of a big win. But as these were the only physical demands placed upon us, candy floss proved to be the ideal form of sustenance.

The scent of candy floss was inextricably fused with the equally pungent and pervasive smell of diesel–powered generators on which the fair's whole spectacle crucially depended. As an insatiably curious small–time adventurer I would sometimes turn off the main, crowded path, and soon find myself alone, underneath, and behind a ride. Here, backstage as it were, I could peer into the dark belly of the fairground's beasts and make out the shadowy shapes of their greasy apparatus. The fearsome cogs that made the ride whirl, roll, spin or whip reeked of oil, and so the scent of candy floss would be supplanted, just as music pumping out above was cancelled by the close proximity of noisy generators. Even as the introspective youth I was then, I sensed on such occasions the importance of turning away like this, avoiding the main spectacle and purposefully 'missing the point'. Only then could I gain access to a certain sovereign privilege, witness certain secrets, and thereby understand dark forces that made possible the fairground's fervid fantasy and froth.

Even as a sparely educated teenager I soberly calculated how important it might be to appreciate the energetic consumption and material base on which the fair's fun relied. Behind every sparkling watt and uplifting decibel a less attractive engineering feat was being executed every time a drip of oil was spilt, sacrificed, and sent–up as smoke to obscure the stars.

By means of such meditative empirical expeditions I began to feel increasingly informed concerning the merits and secrets of my life in modernity. I sensed that I was a relatively powerless punter, part of an un–propertied, far from wealthy family, born at — or close to — the bottom of a nervously balanced socio–economic ladder. I was starting–out by starting to look up and all around, hoping for a worthwhile life, yet knowing I could never expect to have one handed to me.

Nevertheless, I did not know that several decades could and would be spent negotiating with the noisy cornucopia of disorientating enticements proffered by various, more or less reputable hucksters, each out for my buck, time, youth and attention. I gradually learned that my chances of enjoying life's longer, larger, ride, without being too furiously flayed or rapidly fleeced, would ultimately rely on my very own way of thinking, some internal savvy, personal ways and means of seeing and doing, and eventually — some way down the line — a little education too.

Looking back now, it seems that, in order to confront, contest, or attempt to conquer the bank–rolled powers and energy–resourced workings of the greater world market, and the empire of enforced entertainment that dominates and levitates all of our post–modern lives, it helped me to, there and then explore the workings of those greasy cogs and wheels, thundering away, hidden to most and for most of the time, powering the procession of colourful appearances spinning and gliding, swaying and bumping above.

Henceforth, throughout my life, and for a while encouraged by the loyal companionship of photography,[2] I found that empowering personal insights, and clarification of my own way of thinking, might be best acquired when actively cultivating a private perspective that feels licensed to look up–close, behind, beneath and occasionally awry, at the given. Furthermore, while savouring initially optical episodes I thereby learned to have adventures with ideas,[3] following those too along narrow lanes, over stiles, or considering their own forking paths. I have not ceased to take increasingly curious interest in the significance of

2. O'Kane, P. (2014). Theme of my previous **eeodo** publication *Where Is That Light Now?*

3. Whitehead, A. N. (1943). Echoing the wonderfully titled *Adventures of Ideas*. First published 1933.

my immediate surroundings and everyday experiences, all the while unashamedly acknowledging, monitoring, *my* own narrative, *my* place and role in the world, refusing to be just a duped and dumbed–down client for another's shady trade, but rather acting as observer, reporter and recorder, one who *takes* themselves and all they see a little more seriously, and who hopes, by way of some deep–seated belief in fair exchange, to thereby *give* a little assistance to the progress of this faltering world.

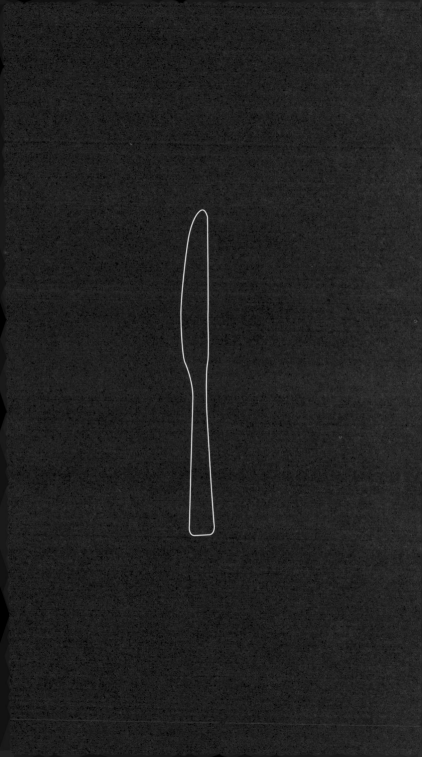

MOVING
ACCIDENTS

Jean Baudrillard once stated: "Even the cinema cultivates the myth of slow motion and the freeze–frame as moments highest drama".[1] The image of slow motion appears to occupy a position somewhere on a sliding scale *between* the moving and the still, and thus might offer some sense of what is at stake in the relation of motion and narrative.

Walter Benjamin was also struck by the way a close–up still, or slowed–down moving image seems to open–up a previously unseen and thus unknown realm in which the most quotidian of acts take on a mystique that demands and deserves our renewed consideration, contemplation or even meditation.[2]

The words 'slow motion' however, appear in a Romantic poem some time before they could become applied to the new image–technologies of film and video. In the *Lyrical Ballads* of 1802 Wordsworth had already coined, or at least used the phrase in the first lines of the poem *Hart Leap Well*:[3]

The Knight had ridden down from Wensley Moor
With the slow motion of a summer's cloud;
He turn'd aside towards a Vassal's door,
And 'Bring another Horse!' he cried aloud.

Wordsworth then begins part two of the same poem using

---

1.   Baudrillard, J. (1993). p. 155.

2.   Benjamin, W. (1968). pp. 235–237. T*he Work of Art in the Age of Mechanical Reproduction*, Section XIII.

3.   Stafford, F. (2013). p. 203–206.

the related phrases — "moving accident" and "freeze the blood":

The moving accident is not my trade:
To freeze the blood I have no ready arts:
'Tis my delight, alone in summer shade,
To pipe a simple song for thinking hearts.

While "slow motion" may have been coined by Wordsworth, the source for "moving accident" can be traced to Shakespeare's *Othello* where it seems to refer to the actions of a knight or warrior in the full flow of battle. In *Hart Leap Well*, Wordsworth is saying such warlike actions are "not my trade", i.e. not the actions of a poet, or at least not the actions of the new kind of Romantic poet he has professed to be in the Preface to *Lyrical Ballads*. A Romantic poet may nevertheless be interested in accidents of a sort, even while behaving far from violently. Thus the next stanza reads:

As I from Hawes to Richmond did repair,
It chanc'd that I saw standing in a Dell
Three Aspins at three corners of a square,
And one, not four yards distant, near a Well.

The Romantic poet enjoys, plays with, and perhaps comes to revere such 'chance' as a privileged moment, something sudden, but not fearful so as to "freeze the blood". Rather, the arresting moment singles out a significant image from ongoing experience, one that deserves to be recorded. It is a gift from the benign force of chance as a modern god perhaps, or compensation for the lost God).

It is a momentary image rescued from the motion of a wayward perambulation.

Looking at Shakespeare's *Othello* in detail we find (within the story of the telling of the story of a life) "moving accidents" and also "disastrous chances":

OTHELLO:[4]

Her father loved me, oft invited me,
Still questioned me the story of my life
From year to year — the battles, sieges, fortunes
That I have passed.
I ran it through, even from my boyish days
To th' very moment that he bade me tell it,[5]
Wherein I spoke of most disastrous chances,
Of moving accidents by flood and field,
Of hair–breadth scapes i' th' imminent deadly
    breach,
Of being taken by the insolent foe
And sold to slavery; of my redemption thence
And portance in my travailous history;
Wherein of antres vast and deserts idle,
Rough quarries, rocks, hills whose heads touch
    heaven

---

4. Shakespeare, W. (2004). *Othello*. 1.3.130

5. "I ran it through, even from my boyish days/ To th' very moment that he bade me tell it". Such narrative circularity invokes, and may perhaps have inspired Barthes' interpretation (in *The Death of the Author*) of Proust's great experimental life–novel as an iniquitously self–reflexive book that takes hundreds of pages and numerous volumes to reach the point (the end) at which that very same book, that the reader has just finished reading, can finally start to be written (the beginning). It also brings us echoes of Scheherazade.

It was my hint to speak — such was my process —
And of the Cannibals that each other eat, . . .

Among knights, warriors, battles, horses, slavery and chance; between Othello, Wordsworth, Shakespeare and Benjamin, we have here set out a panoply of reference related to the context of romance and Romanticism. Knights and warriors writhe, twist and leap in battle, but only as do avatars operated by today's X Box gamers as they virtually progress through simulated ordeals towards some more or less attainable, more or less mythic or romantic goal, often, of course, through the explicitly Romantic scenario of a sublime–looking virtual landscape.[6] Skill, strength, discipline and determination might all be required, both for the real and the virtual warrior, but chance or accident will also need to be considered, even courted, playing, as they do, significant parts in the making of any victory, whether it be the achievement of the poet, the warrior or the gamer. A romantic needs chance on their side.

When jazz maestro Miles Davis once proclaimed "there are no mistakes"[7] he surely meant, not that he, the world, or history were perfect but that he had learned (like Othello) to accommodate chance into his virtuosic mastery of musicianship. Deaf to the nay sayers, he played, like the warrior who incorporates and affirms every "moving accident…" and "hair–breadth scapes i' th' imminent deadly breach", to thereby innovate and incorporate all

---

6. Contemporary artist Jon Rafman has produced ample video–collaged and curated evidence of a certain techno–Romanticist aesthetic almost endemic within computer video game design.

7. Apocryphal, but nevertheless irresistible.

into his technique (or technology); into the tale of his every performance and that of his overall career. The audacious, quick–witted warrior, the skilled musician, the avid gamer, as well as the gentle poet, might all then be said to 'make their own luck', an ability which, though born perhaps more of determination than skill, puts them on a par and in a seamless dialogue with those gods who once embodied chance or served us our fortune in mysterious ways.

The conscious acknowledgement of chance in Wordsworth's poem denotes a Romantic willingness to relinquish human control over fate and experience, thereby reducing the conscious power and presence of the self in order to place experience in the hands of, and perhaps on a par with motion and change, as inexorable, immanent forces.

Nature, in its sublime manifestation, is that over which we cannot exert control. Yet chance is an apparently natural force, a way for us to access, approximate, or return to nature, a facility by means of which we might rally some dialogue with those natural forces that lie both within and without us and from which modernity appears to distance us.

If chance is natural it may nevertheless be one Romantic trace that we can transport into the city and thus into modern life. Sigmund Freud, and Freudian Surrealism, emphasised this facility or potential, directly addressing the interplay of humanity, nature, chance, rationality, science, superstition, myth, and the gods. Freud built *parapraxes* into his modern science of the unconscious while

Breton built automatism into his theory of art.

The sky darkens inexorably, beyond our power to resist. We might light a candle or switch–on a lamp for assurance, perhaps boot–up a backlit laptop powered by electricity from some distant, surging river, funnelled through a dam. The weather turns and we note our subjection to meteorological shifts. Our mood might swing on a passing cloud. Thus embroiled within nature we are reminded of our own condition as climatic creatures, each our own weather system, only as modern as we are also natural beings.

The early modern arts, and the aesthetics of Romanticism may generally be considered a response to, and a refusal of increasing and encroaching technological hubris. Romanticism is a willingness, and perhaps a need, to maintain a certain modesty, empathy, humility, mystery and fragile sensitivity, to balance an increasingly robust, technologised and unnatural epoch marked out by an all–too–human and yet also all–too–inhumane industrial revolution, a revolution which is, in its turn, accompanied by the growing confidence and ascendancy of rational, scientific thought in modern society.

While Walter Benjamin marveled at revelations provided by slow motion cinema images, he was also embracing the model of the *flâneur*, that knight of modernity, scion of street and arcade, who is as much perambulatory poet as cultural warrior, and who will also accrue sufficient influence for these two figures to be combined in the emerging model of the critical theorist, a brave commentator on everyday phenomena, as poetic as political, and as theological as philosophical.

It is worth here quoting Benjamin at length in a passage that seems to lie close to the heart of this project:

"By close–ups of the things around us, by focusing on hidden details of familiar objects, by exploring common place *milieus* under the ingenious guidance of the camera, the film, on the one hand, extends our comprehension of the necessities which rule our lives; on the other hand, it manages to assure us of an immense and unexpected field of action. Our taverns and our metropolitan streets, our offices and furnished rooms, our railroad stations and our factories appeared to have us locked up hopelessly. Then came the film and burst this prison–world asunder by the dynamite of the tenth of a second, so that now, in the midst of its far–flung ruins and debris, we calmly and adventurously go travelling. With the close–up, space expands; with slow motion, movement is extended. The enlargement of a snapshot does not simply render more precise what in any case was visible, though unclear: it reveals entirely new structural formations of the subject. So, too, slow motion not only presents familiar qualities of movement but reveals in them entirely unknown ones 'which, far from looking like retarded rapid movements, give the effect of singularly gliding, floating, supernatural motions'. Evidently a different nature opens itself to the camera than opens to the naked eye — if only because an unconsciously penetrated space is substituted for a space consciously explored by man. Even if one has a general knowledge of the way people walk, one knows nothing of a person's posture during the fractional second of a stride. The act of reaching for a lighter or a spoon is familiar routine, yet we hardly know what really goes on between hand and metal, not to mention how this fluctuates with our moods. Here the camera intervenes with the resources of its lowerings and liftings,[8] its interruptions and isolations, its extensions and accelerations, its enlargements and reductions. The camera introduces us to unconscious optics as does psychoanalysis to unconscious impulses".[9]

Benjamin's interwar critical theory embraces the poetic vision of the *flâneur* while becoming embroiled in a creative interpretation of the everyday, to the extent that, in the quote above he is contemplating the quotidian close–up and slowed–down in a detailed technological image, while poetically evaluating — and thereby romanticising, humanising — the very latest technology. This is perhaps the kind of creative perspective we need to take today, scrutinising, both imaginatively and critically the new technologies of our own times, to thereby see what they may be able to reveal about ourselves and our world that we did not previously realise. All too often new technologies are deployed to merely exacerbate, exponentially multiply, and thereby consolidate the familiar.

Benjamin often constructs historical continuities, not merely assuming to project a forward thinking line of thought as a linear modernist but thinking more

8. Vertov. D. (2000). Dziga Vertov's self–reflexive (1929) film *Man With A Movie Camera* appears to be invoked here.

9. Benjamin, W. (1968). pp. 217–251. *The Work of Art in the Age of Mechanical Reproduction*, Section XIII.

holistically and in all directions, even mapping the advent of ideas as what he calls 'constellations'. An idea, as constellation, is briefly convened by chance and memory as it objectifies and shares a convergence momentarily formed by a subjective and perspectival parallax, and as the subject entertains and enjoys the relativity and contingency of more than one coinciding reference arising from the particular chaotic and complex stimuli of the modern environment. Benjamin also appears to trace this very activity to Romanticism's evolution out of certain threads and remnants of the thought of Immanuel Kant.[10]

In Benjamin, the new, immediate, and present invokes and encounters the old, remote and deferred. No crude and simple line is drawn between present, future and past, between modernity and history, between the modern and traditional. Benjamin eagerly inherited Baudelaire's nineteenth century amalgam of Romanticism, Symbolism and Realism, by means of which the modern poet or thinker is able to perpetuate a mode of thought that reaches back at least as far as medieval literature, and further, implicating the humble, wandering Roma as much as the chivalric knight or Rome's tidal empire.

Here we can glimpse an evocative, emotive and affective seam, mined by Benjamin throughout a tragically curtailed career and according to which history becomes a poetic subject, an affective and sensuous dialogue with time, shared no less by the contingent rhythms of linked syllables than by the palimpsests of supposedly distinct

10. Hanssen, B. & Benjamin, A. (Eds.). (2002).

epochs.

Poetry and history are thus both forms of motion study, studies *of* motion made *in* motion (hence the backward–facing stance and irresistible propulsion of Benjamin's 'angel of history').[11] History and poetry are both ways of understanding lives in the world in motional and emotive, as much as technical, analytical and scientific terms.

History is culture convincingly composed in rhetorical, rhythmic, gracious and ornate fashion.[12] Now we are modern we can view and review history in close–up, slow or fast motion, brush it either with or against the grain (neither of which will be any truer or more accurate). Poetry meanwhile, as it can be said to be a primarily and fundamentally mnemonic device, is equally and innately archival, and thus merely the continuation of history by other means.[13]

11. Benjamin, W. (1968). pp. 253–264.

12. Of course fashion itself may be (along perhaps with changes in popularly adopted gestures) history's most ubiquitous, and simultaneously most natural (i.e. seasonal), un–theorisable and mysterious face.

13. Eliot, T. S. (1981). Eliot would surely agree.

KUMIKO THE TREASURE HUNTER

Kumiko The Treasure Hunter,[1] a 2014 film directed by David Zellner, begins with the lone figure of a young woman on a beach. She is using a rudimentary, hand–made map. On entering a cave, she finds, buried within, a weathered VHS videotape. It turns out to be *Fargo*, a hit movie made in 1996 by left–of–field Hollywood directors The Coen Brothers. Importantly, their film begins with the official–looking proviso: "THIS IS A TRUE STORY".[2]

Driven by some maverick intuition that we never fully understand (a little like the obsession of Richard Dreyfuss' character in Stephen Spielberg's 1977 film *Close Encounters of the Third Kind*)[3] Kumiko gradually deconstructs her boring and predictable Tokyo lifestyle and sets out on a recklessly romantic adventure, the aim of which is to retrieve a horde of cash visible in the closing scene of *Fargo* as it is buried under snow on the border wilderness of Minnesota, USA, by Steve Buscemi's character.

As frustration with her banal environment, and commitment to her unlikely project grow, Kumiko walks out of her job, destroys her SIM card, and funds a trip to America with her boss's credit card (at least until it is cancelled). She stubbornly and clumsily overcomes all obstacles and every affront to her strangely romantic, irrational quest, which she compares with the historical activities of "conquistadors".

---

1.   Zellner, D. (Director). (2014).

2.   Coen. J. (Director). (1996).

3.   Spielberg, S. (Director). (1977).

All help offered or provided by sensible, well–meaning people encountered on her way is roundly rejected. A kind policeman repeatedly tells her that the scene from *Fargo*, on which she has hinged her romantic goal, is "fake". But this only provokes emotional exasperation in Kumiko who consequently rejects his companionship and goes it alone.

The conclusion of the film and its plot is left slightly am-biguous. One reading could be that Kumiko in fact — and realistically — dies of the cold after stumbling around in an unknown land, ill–prepared for Minnesota's hostile climate, wrapped in a motel duvet. Thus the film could be the tragic documentation of a fatal nervous breakdown, exacerbated by an obsessive and overly subjective dia-logue with media. However, even if this is the case, and if this is the film's ultimate reality, it is nevertheless sub-ordinated to an apparently happier ending that may bet-ter please and satisfy the viewer's desires. The explicitly presented conclusion sees Kumiko awaken from a snowy mound (though this of course could be the dream or hallucination of a dying girl), then correctly identify and arrive at the place where Buscemi, in the Coen Brothers' movie, buried his treasure.

Furthermore, she finds there, not an ironic plot twist but simply the case filled with thousands of dollars that she had always truly believed to be there. She is also reunited — inexplicably, impossibly, magically — with the cute pet that she discarded on the Tokyo underground before travelling to America.

If we take this to be the actual end of the story, the fact that Kumiko seems to have been right all along makes her, not only justified in romantically and unrealistically pursuing, at all costs, her subjective intuition, it also means that she becomes immediately wealthy and independent enough to reconcile her own reality with the reality of those others whom she has disturbed, offended, rejected and stolen from, in order to reach her personal goal and fulfil her own belief.

All the social, moral and financial debts accumulated through the course of her troublesome, transgressive and apparently insane actions can now be repaid, not at any other point in her narrative but only in the final moment of its realisation. The cash — like all buried treasure, in all such stories — may be a modern stand–in for the pre–modern legend of a Holy Grail.

This ending, though by definition unrealistic, may nevertheless give the audience an elated sense of reassurance, that irrational pursuits, idiosyncratic beliefs, and unrealistic goals should or must be allowed to play themselves out, and do have a place in our lives, despite so much post–modern irony arising from an increasing sense of complicity with incarceral consumerist comfort and conformity.

Some effective form of romance does, and should have a place in our lives, our world, our identity, our politics and our aspirations. Given an opportunity to become realised, unlikely possibilities; possibility *per se;* even dreams might be able or allowed to come true. Magic, of a kind, might just work. To make art we invariably have to pursue an intuition that leads us (awkwardly, uncomfortably, arduously, patiently) and (if we are fortunate) also delivers us, beyond that which we had previously believed was possible for us, for others, and also for art. It may thus be that art, combined with technology, is able to provide something indistinguishable from magic, despite the continuous nay saying of rationality, irony, logic, likelihood, stats and facts.[4]

Making the apparently impossible possible (one definition of magic) could be a more romantic way of framing socio–economic aspirations to greater equality, as, for various reasons (e.g. wealth, power, status, class, connection, technology, access, knowledge, location or ability) what is possible for one person, one society, or one epoch may be impossible for another.

Friedrich Nietzsche's own brand of Romantic philosophy had, at its heart, an affirmation of affirmation itself. He thus saw what he called "nay sayers" as enemies of his vibrant philosophy of life. Some sense of this Nietzschean approach might be illustrated by Kumiko's own intuitive — albeit possibly insane — sense of romance, opposed

4. E.g. in a recently overheard broadcast discussion between someone of a Left wing political viewpoint and someone of a Right wing viewpoint, the Left wing thinker made her points while repeatedly apologising for her own vision as 'perhaps idealistic but ...' and 'utopian but...' Meanwhile, the Right wing thinker politely refrained from damning the other while nevertheless repeatedly saying (and implicitly inviting the Left wing thinker to concur) 'but it's not going to happen' or 'but it's not going to happen in our lifetimes'. The Republican, ex–presidential candidate (in 2008) Sarah Palin also comes to mind, describing, in a 2010 speech, Obama's (as well as the Democrats' and the Left in general's) political belief system as: "that hopey, changey stuff".

by the nay sayers who surround her as they insist upon playing by the rules, living out prescribed and predictable lives, resigning themselves to safety, compromise, and compliance with a narrow–minded and delimiting society. They make their own, all–too clear–cut distinctions between reality and unreality, and insist that certain things are possible, manageable and desirable while others are certainly not.

Nevertheless, as we mentioned above, a certain, perhaps necessary ambiguity suggests that the joyful closing scene of *Kumiko The Treasure Hunter* may in fact be the dream or vision of a dead, or dying and deluded young woman who has been reduced by a nervous breakdown to a slow death, far from home, in a hostile blizzard.

From the first frames until the last, this movie keeps our idea of the true, the mythic, the magical, the sane and insane in a special balance. We are left to decide whether we continue to buy–in to a modern rationality, a post–modern theory of simulacra, a Magical Realism, or something else, something twenty first century perhaps that does not sit comfortably with any of the above.

The varying technologies that play their part in this film are helpful to consider. We first encounter a hand–sewn map. There is also a page torn from an atlas, as well as a state map of Minnesota proffered at the airport. These concur with Kumiko's careful mapping, directly on her TV monitor, of the crucial scene from *Fargo*. Then there is the ailing, failing VHS tape and its troubled player. When both of these break, the unspooled VHS tape is unceremoniously flushed down a toilet, eventually to be supplanted by a DVD version of the film. There is also the Coen Brothers' movie *Fargo*, itself a technology made by and for a previous generation of movie fans. Then we have a mobile phone and its SIM card, a credit card, an airliner, various land line telephones, two or three cars, a pair of stout boots and a duvet that becomes a ritual-istic, regal–looking cloak for the final stage of Kumiko's quasi–mythical adventure.

How do these technologies influence the romance, or affect the narrative plot? All play an intrinsic part in ena-bling and motivating the protagonist, but what then is the overarching significance of this array of historical tech-nologies as they play their various parts in Kumiko's sto-ry? To be able to travel rapidly from Tokyo to Minnesota requires a jet airliner. Meanwhile a credit card obliterates financial barriers that might make the journey, and thus the story, impossible.[5] Like many stories, this one relies closely upon the model of the journey itself. It is the story of a journey, and the story is also a journey.

The mobile phone and its SIM card suffer an early de-mise, perhaps because, to Kumiko, they allow for and encourage the constant encroachment of other voices, other realities that might challenge her own increasingly unequivocal and determined subjectivity. Friends, family and employer (all of whom might contact Kumiko via the

---

5.   The expropriation by the female employee of the male employer's money
     to enable the adventure is an echo of Hitchcock's (1960) movie *Psycho*,
     a connection which also suggests feminist, anti–patriarchal (as well as
     Freudian, Lacanian, Žižek–ian) readings of Kumiko's tale.

phone) represent the normal life, logic, facts and reality that, to Kumiko, seem devoid of meaningful narrative, bereft of any romance or goal that is as personal, idiosyncratic, specific, ambitious, enjoyable and as interesting as the retrieving of buried treasure on the other side of the world. By comparison with Kumiko's own romance the ways of life of others appear meaningless. Meaning and value, for Kumiko, lie, if not actually in the past then in some symbolic dialogue with the past — an old film, near–redundant VHS technology, the concept of treasure, and the conquistadors with whom she compares herself.

For a sensible consumer the assurance of attaining the suburban dream necessarily lies in a vague, elusive, but necessarily plausible near–future, the convenient and prescribed time–frame on which modern, capitalist lifestyles and politicians' promises depend. Life plans, careers, insurance policies and pensions vaguely obfuscate the inevitable prospect of death and supplant any sense of life as a truly unpredictable adventure, thus playing into the hands and complying with the logic of an overarching, exploitative, economic system.

Any publicised image of social and economic stability however belies the casino–like, risk–based machinations of the marketplace on which a capitalist society is precariously balanced. A misleading image of conformity, complicity and stability legitimates and justifies the increasingly incarceral, prescribed existence of humdrum, salaried employments who's carefully calculated and parsimoniously delimited rewards are sucked, as rapidly as possible (often immediately, even pre–emptively) back into the market in return for compensatory comforts, commodified goods and services. All of this is celebrated and promoted as an unparalleled and interminable festival of choice and desire.

Common sense, objectivity, logic and meaning rely upon generic, objective, manageable goals, the pursuit of which, we are promised, will, if we are fortunate, improve our lot and take us closer to an ideal portrayed by advertising, movies and other media. However, this system insists on imposing repetition and stability only to extract a regular and consistent supply of predictable profitability from our human daily needs and spirited wishes. It thereby refuses, denies and suppresses any significant transformation, threat, or challenge to its own overarching paradigm i.e. the capitalist, consumerist system, which even attempts to render our society ahistorical and thus devoid of its own, and consequently our own, narrative adventure (or romance).

The current political generation appears to face the prospect of a life lived without appeal to any alternative or oppositional political narrative, indeed, without narrative *per se*. The dominant system would have us, rather, transfixed in a state of perpetual fascination, like creatures with our faces glued to tiny, hand–held vending machines.

Living in one of the wealthiest and most technologically advanced societies on earth, Kumiko divests herself of her economic structure and turns to the past, in various ways, to find an alternative to, or escape from her society's prescribed, systemised and imposed lifestyles. This doesn't necessarily make Kumiko someone who lives in the past, in the modern sense that has come to sound pejorative, and as might e.g. also have been applied to Don Quixote. Rather she is trying, desperately, to find a way where there is presently no way. She is trying to find a way forwards, out, and beyond, and in this she is living and thinking historically.

Consumerism, while exploiting the retro just as successfully as any other mineral resource or revenue stream, nevertheless frames it as new and fixates us on the new, particularly on the newest technology. However, art writer, academic and curator Nicholas Bourriaud claimed that, for a world whose entire surface is either snapped by Google or daily scrutinised by orbiting satellites, history becomes "the last continent to be discovered".[6] He thus exposes the same space of possibility that Kumiko seems to access in this movie by using the past, in various ways, as a means of escape and of locating possibility.

Kumiko chooses, in the images of conquistador and treasure, and in the unreality afforded by the slightly outmoded technology of cinema (referred to in both the VHS format and the DVD manifestations of *Fargo*) to believe wholeheartedly in what the friendly policeman character (played by the film's director) nevertheless tells her is "fake".

---

6. Bourriaud, N. (Ed.). (2009). *Altermodern* (essay). No page numbers, however see latter part of first section *'The Figure In The Carpet' The Tale of an Exhibition*.

The philosopher of simulation, Jean Baudrillard, hyperbolically, and provocatively claimed that America depends upon Disneyland to provide the rest of America with the sense that it is real, that it is other to, and at least not as unreal as Disneyland.[7] Similarly, *Kumiko The Treasure Hunter* seems to aim to expose the scene at the end of the movie *Fargo* as playing some part at least in the maintenance of the reality we return to when *Fargo* is over, once we have left the cinema or ejected the DVD.

Kumiko's insistence that this fake has to be real (remember that *Fargo* begins with the proviso "THIS IS A TRUE STORY") sustains and restores to her life the crucial resources of adventure, romanticism, meaning and value, along with invention, history, and the idiosyncratic craft signified by her hand–sewn cloth maps.

It may be important to interject here an as–yet overlooked political or social aspect of *Kumiko The Treasure Hunter*. Though written, directed and produced by Americans, the story is nevertheless told as a Japanese response to a heavily Americanised culture. American culture was imposed upon Japan and many Asian countries and cultures in the wake of America's 'victory' in WW2. Japan's response is also well known. For several decades following the war, and having initially resented the intrusion of American society and values, Japan built an unequalled reputation for unprecedented productivity, inventing new products, while improving on, reducing the cost and increasing the profitability of what in many cases were originally

---

7. Baudrillard, J. (1983). *Hyperreal & Imaginary.* pp. 23–26.

American goods, American modes of manufacture and distribution.

In this way Japan became a pioneer of late twentieth century global economics, coming to supplant American monopolies and, according to the competitive logic of the capitalist market, to challenge accepted notions of national loyalty to home–grown brands and goods, thereby instigating proto–globalisation as well as an accompanying culture of proto–post–modernism. (Interestingly, in light of our wider concern here, Japanese goods were often derided as fakes or poor copies by Europeans and Americans loyal to long–standing national brands).

As Japan, along with much of 'liberated' and vanquished Asia, was catapulted into becoming an Americanised, globally ascendant, economic and technological power, Japanese mainstream culture as well as abundant new subcultures emerging within its dynamic and youthful post WW2 society, cultivated an adventurous, speculative and ironic response to the accelerated surrender of its traditional, spiritual, religious and social values.[8] A reading of the works of author and activist Yukio Mishima[9] help articulate and historicise the tensions pervading and informing Japan's rapid twentieth century transformation. Mishima initially recorded tensions between modernisation and traditional lifestyles and values but gradually developed into a more decadent, narcissistic, post–modern version of himself, before finally, all–too–fascistically,

---

8.   Judt, T. (2005). pp. 102, 280–282, 597.

9.   Mishima, Y. (2000)., Mishima, Y. (2000) (b)., and Mishima, Y. (2001).

fatally, and Romantically (in perhaps the worst sense of the word) lamenting, Japan's loss of traditional, auratic, mythical and hierarchical power.

It could be argued that, for Kumiko's generation, a passionate, historically and ideologically driven writer like Mishima has been supplanted by Haruki Murakami,[10] a globally best–selling novelist, essayist and short–story writer who invites and allows what is described as Magical Realism to pervade his work. A taste for and awareness of Magical Realism may at least inform *Kumiko The Treasure Hunter* and might also be assumed to have influenced the tastes of a potential audience of young Japanese who could thus find in Kumiko a heroine or role model.

Magical Realism is a literary form also propagated by certain influential and canonic Latin American writers[11] whose cultures and societies have their own uncomfortable relationship with Euro–American postcolonial power. British Indian author Salman Rushdie deployed the genre as a critical and strategic response to a postcolonial condition in which indigenous, traditional, non–modern and non–Euro–American beliefs, logics and realities might be free to propose and promote elements of ancient and alternative narratives, thereby contesting an otherwise hegemonic and potentially totalitarian global power and cultural paradigm.

10. Murakami, H. (2007).

11. Borges, J. L. (1964)., Borges, J. L. (2000)., Borges, J. L. (2002)., Danow, D. K. (1995)., Hart, S. M. & Wen–chin Ouyang, W–c (Eds.). (2010)., and Zamora, L. P. & Wendy B. Faris, W. B.(Eds.). (1995).

Given the above, we might begin to re–interpret *Kumiko The Treasure Hunter* thus: Symbolically, the young Japanese woman travels towards the cold, hard reality and fact of Hollywood's supposedly fake narrative, with the impassioned aim of exposing it as "not fake" but "real". By this means, Kumiko aims to liberate herself, but also, by implication, perhaps to free her own country's traditional culture, along with all countries and cultures under the spell of America's supposedly fake images (which disguise and belie America's reality). America is, after all, all too real. It could kill you. If the wilderness doesn't get you then the automobiles, guns, privatised health system, dearth of welfare or ascendant xenophobia will. A girl could die there.

Meanwhile, *Kumiko The Treasure Hunter* is a movie, and therefore itself fake, not real. However, as a movie–about–a–movie it offers itself as a meta–movie with some claim therefore to another or different, level or layer of plays between fakeness and reality, i.e. other or different at least to the plays of fakeness and reality of the Coen brothers' movie which is its object or referent.

We may seem to be entering a labyrinth of intertwined and overlain fakes and realities here but it is precisely this layering and doubling, this meta–reality and meta–fakery that allows *Kumiko The Treasure Hunter* to suggest or provide the possibility of a rejuvenated romantic approach to art, life and culture, and thereby a possible way out of a cultural impasse.

Notwithstanding Kumiko's own fakeness (as herself

a character in another movie) she insists on pursuing an unrealistic adventure at the real cost of her job, her friends, her home, her family, her pet, her reputation, her economy and her status as a respectable law–abiding citizen. However, in doing so, the character of Kumiko seems to restore our belief in the power of storytelling, and perhaps our belief in the power of a repressed, indigenous, local and traditional form of storytelling (Walter Benjamin would approve) while reclaiming certain intuitive or innate values of romance and magic that have been lost to, expropriated, colonised and monopolised by an external, dominant and oppressive power, the same power that has so comprehensively constructed the capitalist and consumerist lifestyle from which Kumiko is desperate to escape.

As Benjamin says, any story worth telling has something useful to offer, and the storytelling tradition often relies upon travel, if only because travel, precisely by making a story unverifiable and shrouding it in mystique, gives a story a special authority which is other than, and superior to (in Benjamin's opinion) that of information, even if the information is quickly verifiable as factual and true. A story provides something more, and something more useful than information, more than media, facts, stats and even truth, and certainly more useful than the predictable and repetitive chit–chat Kumiko hears at work or from old school friends concerning kids or "permed eyelashes".

The Coen Brothers' *Fargo* is itself of course a sophisticated and ironic form of American movie, made by a progressive post–modern generation, newly self–conscious and reflexive regarding cinema's canon and repertoire of tropes. Their film begins by alerting us with the words "THIS IS A TRUE STORY" but ends with the words "all persons fictitious", provoking controversial critical commentary. After years of issuing varying statements regarding the source and veracity of the film the directors finally stated: "the only thing true about it is that it's a story".

Here we can glimpse some echo of Walter Benjamin's aversion to information and favouring of storytelling. Both could provide a kind of episteme or paradigm for a society, though for Benjamin one appears more attractive and more roundly human than the other. If we become replete with information yet starved of stories, some sense of speculation, risk and adventure in our lives must nevertheless be maintained — and not merely by holiday brokers, car salesmen, or estate agents, who promise fulfilment and adventure only to deliver us to yet another website or another long queue.

Despite reality, despite science, despite facts and despite appearances, romance may not just be a description of a certain kind of narrativity, nor a reference to a historical culture, epoch, or paradigm. It may, rather, be a crucial part of being human, of living a rounded, not merely rational and not merely modern or post–modern life. Like the mythical damsel in distress of chivalric legend, romance itself constantly requires rescue from the dragons of banality, resignation, restriction and complicity.

As the heroine of a meta–movie Kumiko's insistent objection seems to be that *Fargo* is real, must be real, or is, in addition to being a (fake) movie, also real. She sets out, not only to gain the treasure but to simultaneously prove (and the treasure may then be a metaphor for this proving) that Hollywood, despite supposedly playing a similarly assuring role to that accorded Disneyland by Baudrillard, is in fact all too real. Hollywood is real e.g. in the oppressive, monopolistic and hegemonic way it represses international and indigenous storytelling traditions (and, by implications, indigenous culture in general).[12]

We might also suggest that, by striving to prove that the conclusion to *Fargo* is real, Kumiko sets out to prove that Hollywood is insufficiently fake, too real, not escapist enough, not unreal enough, not imaginative or magical enough to sustain this young Japanese woman's passionate need for belief in adventure and romance. Kumiko, like all of us, needs something other than, and more than her workaday (Americanised) reality, to offer her some way to go, imagine, dream and travel beyond the untenable limitations of the kind of prescribed existence that capitalist consumerism deems adequate or acceptable for the expenditure of a human life. The romantic journey she undertakes therefore proves her own reality while simultaneously exposing the fake fakery (*sic*) of Hollywood.

As we suggested above, the ultimate treasure or Holy Grail that Kumiko retrieves at the end of her heroic quest is not thousands of dollars in cash but proof that Hollywood is real, a proof that can only be explained using the particular form of a meta–movie, a palimpsest or doubling that,

12. Cousins, M. (Director). (2012).

by means of juxtaposition and proximity of two movies, two narratives, two takes on reality and fakery, something akin to a *moiré* pattern of magical possibility appears, magical if only because it presents possibilities beyond those previously believed available.

Fargo's opening statement "THIS IS A TRUE STORY" gives Kumiko the cue and the confidence (we might say the audacity) to seek–out and contradict the romance–deficit in her own lifestyle, but also to expose the shortcomings of Hollywood's provision.[13] Like Walter Benjamin, what Kumiko may be looking for is something that is truly a story, and in the end both Kumiko and the Coen Brothers might concur, and celebrate the fact that "the only true thing" about *Fargo* "is that it's a story", "not fake" but real at least in that it is a real story. And that is what Kumiko needs, demands, and, as twenty first century human be-ing, possibly deserves.[14]

Walter Benjamin may have been precocious or prescient to warn of the encroachment of information threatening to crowd–out our ability to tell stories, but the figure of Kumiko, along with the global popularity of Murakami's

---

13. The current success of *La La Land* (Dir. Damien Chazelle, 2016) is — as its title suggests — currently heralded as licensing a new era of heightened escapism in Hollywood's provision.

14. The same could be said for voters in leading nations who appear, to some, to be repeatedly and increasingly voting against their own, logical and long–term interest, but (egged on by Right wing journalism), using the facility of elections, referendums and plebiscites to maintain an expressive sense of narrative, adventure, thrill, power, and risk. Democracy may thus be fast becoming a multiplayer video game, a tendency likely to be exacerbated if/when mass online voting is introduced.

Magical Realist[15] literature, might provide some reassurance that our humanity, our nature (perhaps symbolised in the film by Kumiko's close relationship with her pet) will always seek and find romance, or some form or equivalent of romance; that we will always construct or invent some form of alternative and subjective narrative response to a world, a society, or an individual life that appears to have lost, or to be rapidly losing its way.

Kumiko also demonstrates that we must, and need to, discover and pursue our own romance, whether as an individual, a culture, a community, a political movement or a world. Romance after all — crucially, and perhaps by definition — can or should never be imposed upon us.[16]

Kumiko The Treasure Hunter may be a relatively modest cultural artefact, but through it we may see, as though through a new prism or filter, wider cultural concerns. This was of course the method pursued as critical theory

---

15. Ishiguro, K. (2016)., Beedham, M. (2010)., and Matthews, S. & Groes, S. (Eds.) (2009). Following a long hiatus in his production of highly successful and innovative novels, Kazuo Ishiguro returned to publishing in 2015 with *The Buried Giant*, a surprising switch in style to a form of Tolkien–esque Magical Realism, thus promoting speculation and interpretation about how this insightful and perhaps prescient author may see the changing world today, as well as the current validity and possibilities of literature to expose or comment upon the rapid and shocking changes we are experiencing.

16. Today, as I write this, a cruel and crass nexus, of ascendant Right wing politics with ascendant technological communications, has comprehensively monopolised the notion of a cultural and political narrative as a means by which to gain immense political power. Nevertheless, the political Left (for and from which my energy and creativity is expended here) is, I believe, ultimately equipped, and certainly best equipped, to create, conjure and craft the necessary counter–narratives, counter–images or counter–technologies that are urgently needed to balance, contest and defend the best interests of the world against ominous and obscene, ignorant and blinkered, ultimately nihilistic and self–destructive forces.

by Benjamin and his Frankfurt School colleagues, Kracauer, Adorno *et al.* They thought historically, perceiving philosophical and theological profundities as well as political tendencies in the relatively modest offerings of contemporary popular culture, and even in apparently valueless objects.

Within *Kumiko The Treasure Hunter*'s idiosyncrasies we can tease–out poignant relations between technology and romance, in particular the ability of the technology of cinema (and particularly American cinema) to maintain a hold over our ways and means of believing in narrative, romance and magic. Disney's *Fantasia* (1940), *Snow White* (1937) or *Mary Poppins* (1964) might seem extreme examples of a certain cultural appropriation and monopolisation of narrative, romance and magic,[17] but they are no more–so than recent blockbusters like *Avatar* (2009) or *Gravity* (2013), or productions which purposefully exploit global markets by Disney–fying indigenous myths and legends, e.g. movies based on Chinese, or Native American images, names and narratives.

Jean Baudrillard also proclaimed — using his uniquely convincing, hyperbolic rhetoric — the death of the real. In fact, he made the more dramatic claim that the real has been murdered in a perfect crime.[18] As we have already implied, a world–view, cultural paradigm, or philosophy in which reality, fact and truth no longer play a confident

---

17. Benjamin also responded to the — then relatively new — cultural phenomenon of Mickey Mouse in his writings.

18. Baudrillard, J. (1996)., and Baudrillard, J. (1993).

and central part, also questions the root or source of the previously assumed centrality of the real.

Aided by Kumiko's brave acts (as a heroine she acts on our behalf) we can begin to ask what the relationship between romance, reality and technology might be, what it has been, might be, and how it might serve or suppress us. The fake–ness of Hollywood is ultimately a way of maintaining the credence of our belief in a certain, highly technologised reality (American, consumerist capitalism).

However, to believe unswervingly, not in the fake but in the romantic as real and in the real value of stories (as Kumiko appears to do), may not yet be the same thing as Hollywood's habitual (even if prodigiously inventive) play with reality. Just as Murakami or Rushdie or the Latin American Magical Realists may have deployed their Magical Realism with a strategic, cultural aim, perhaps out of cultural necessity, so Kumiko's trajectory may derive from a need to contest a long–established monopolisation of our innate, ancient and universal human propensity to play with reality, fakery and magic, a propensity which, once considered and examined seriously, appears to be a crucial aspect of our ability to survive — and *Kumiko The Treasure Hunter* is, if nothing else, a story of survival.

NEW MEDIA
— HEIR TO
ROMANTICISM

If Walter Benjamin's *Work of Art in the Age of Mechanical Reproduction* essay is key to any discussion involving technology, art, history and society, then Hito Steyerl's more recent *In Defense of the Poor Image*[1] serves a similar purpose for a new generation. Steyerl's essay could be described as an update on the Benjamin original. Not only does Steyerl refer to DVDs, JPEGs, GIFs and WAVs as proletarian, she also evaluates them within a hierarchy of image technologies, just as Benjamin did for photography and cinema. In making their provocative re–evaluations, both writers refer to a certain cultural status that verges on the illicit. Steyerl's DVDs might be pirated, her files ripped, copied and distributed without respect for their originator.

There is something, not only proletarian, subcultural and illicit about these images and references but also marginal and perhaps *avant–garde*. If we think of *avant–gardism* as a fundamental aspect of the modern artist's persona, and if we consider the failure of the *avant–garde* as definitive, illustrative, or causal of post–modernism, then this attribution of an *avant–garde* value to emerging technologies (a kind of personification) rather than to artists themselves, is worth pursuing. [2]

We might also try to account for a proposition that modern *avant–gardism* has roots in Romanticism. Consider

---

1.   Steyerl, H. (2012). pp. 31–45.

2.   Grassmuck, V. (2016). Volker Grassmuck, author of **eeodo** publication *"I'm Alone, But Not Lonely"* also attributes *avant–garde* characteristics to the *otaku* of post–modern Japan.

Coleridge and Wordsworth's *Lyrical Ballads*,[3] a collection of poems that required a special preface, taking the form of both a proto–manifesto and a proviso designed to enable understanding, recognition, and justify the ensuing collection of words as a new, modern poetry. Note also that Benjamin, in his essay on Surrealism[4] insisted upon that crucially *avant–garde* movement's connections with and roots within Romantic poetry (Lautréamont, Rimbaud, Apollinaire, Aragon).

It is a Romantic spirit of courageous, vertiginous, imaginative speculation and invention that comes to manifest itself as *avant–gardism*, first in the Baudelairean call for a modern, or *more* modern art (along with new heroism, new beauty and new emotions), and then in various answers to this call, coming from individual artists like Manet and Courbet but also in new isms, generated by organised collectives and collaborations (Impressionism, Fauvism etc.) hell–bent upon gambling away established values to enable a dynamic futurity to flourish.

Impressionism, initially appearing to disrupt established values in art, appears today to have rescued painting from the age of the steam train and the photograph and delivered it safely into the arms of the future, *this* future, our very own time in which it enjoys a retirement languishing amid scarves, pillowcases and biscuit tins. Nevertheless, we must note that modern art and the *avant–garde* are not simply a perpetuation of Romanticism but the result

3. Stafford, F. (2013).
4. Benjamin, W. (2000). pp. 225–229.

of a particular twist or buckle in Romanticism's dramatic mission.

Benjamin called Rimbaud's *Une Saison en Enfer* "the first document of the (Surrealist) movement" and in support of this claim made much of a small comment written by Rimbaud himself in the margin of the poet's own copy of his book. Benjamin writes:[5]

"Can the point at issue be more definitively and incisively presented than by Rimbaud himself in his personal copy of the book? In the margin, beside the passage 'on the silk of the seas and the arctic flowers', he later wrote, 'There's no such thing'".

Benjamin's interest here seems to be that Rimbaud's dry and decisive comment, rather than his imaginative and metaphorical poem, points to the emergence of a modern, *avant–garde* and post–Romantic sensibility, while not omitting the implication that one grows out of the other in some organic or dialectical fashion. Other comments by Benjamin further clarify the distinction and twist that he perceives as forming an *avant–garde* poetry out of the influence of a Romantic poetry:

"Breton declared his intention of breaking with a praxis that presents the public with the literary precipitate of a certain form of existence while withholding that existence itself".

The *avant–garde* will no longer tease the audience and

5.   Benjamin, W. (2000). pp. 225–229.

withhold a coded value as might the artist and poet in a more Romantic or Classical manner.

"Stated more briefly and dialectically, this means that the sphere of poetry was here explored from within by a closely knit circle of people pushing the 'poetic life' to the utmost limits of possibility".

Life and poetry converge as never before for the *avant–garde* **and in Surrealism.**

"Everything with which it came into contact was integrated. Life only seemed worth living where the threshold between waking and sleeping was worn away in everyone as by the steps of multitudinous images flooding back and forth, language only seemed itself where, sound and image, image and sound interpenetrated with automatic precision and such felicity that no chink was left for the penny–in–the–slot called 'meaning' ".

Again, a certain separation of art and life is breaking down in the twist from Romanticism to Surrealism. Furthermore, meaning ceases to be the *raison d'être* **of poetry and art. The ends or purposes of art and poetry have become less clear.**

"Image and language take precedence. Saint–Pol Roux, retiring to bed about daybreak, fixes a notice on his door: 'Poet at work'. Breton notes: 'Quietly. I want to pass where no one yet has passed, quietly! 'After you, dearest language'. Language takes precedence. Not only before meaning. Also before the self'.

The artist is left behind by image and by language. Now we are merely vehicles, automatons, serving, delivering images and language on their behalf. Poetry works while we sleep.

"This is not the place to give an exact definition of Surrealist experience. But anyone who has perceived that the writings of this circle are not literature but something else 'demonstrations, watchwords, documents, bluffs, forgeries if you will, but at any rate not literature' will also know, for the same reason, that the writings are concerned literally with experiences, not with theories and still less with phantasms. And these experiences are by no means limited to dreams, hours of hashish eating, or opium smoking. It is a cardinal error to believe that, of 'Surrealist experiences', we know only the religious ecstasies or the ecstasies of drugs".

Experience *per se* supersedes literature. Thus a kind of immanence supersedes representation. (And perhaps this is always a temporary victory, a breakthrough, for a new art over an existing regime of representation, an *avant–garde* battle that repeatedly has to be re–fought). The intoxicated experience is also not privileged over other experiences.

"… the true creative overcoming of religious illumination certainly does not lie in narcotics. It resides in a profane illumination…"

Indeed, the ordinary supplants the extraordinary, the commonplace triumphs over the exception. Here Benjamin has further explained that *avant–garde* poetics are not imaginative and metaphorical separations of experience and its representation but rather a kind of immanent convergence wherein any such clear separation is annulled. Henceforth language leads, the poet politely follows, or merely makes a way for language to intratextualise across every dimension and in all directions.

Today's technologies have recently come in from that inevitably cold zone in which new technologies are invariably forced to await any aesthetic validation that places them above and beyond a merely utilitarian value. Recently, the art of the microprocessor has established a realm for itself as new media. Along with Steyerl, numerous theorists now produce new media commentaries, gradually familiarising us with the particular values and possibilities of the latest technologies as vehicles for art. But this follows a generation in which digital art and new media occupied a relatively barren margin and maintained a radical, political, threatening and provocative sense of innovation, of which only the hacker remains as a kind of anti–aesthetic figure of anarchic, hi–tech resistance, informing or inspiring would–be radical new media practices.

One of Walter Benjamin's most valued contributions is the way in which he presciently saw, in and for his own day, the way in which the new media of photography and cinema, as well as the radio and gramophone, occupied a similar position to that currently or recently occupied by our own new media, i.e. somewhere between hobby, entertainment, gimmick, pastime, science and popular art. His most famous essay is, in part, a means by which to assert the opinion that photography and cinema are, or will soon be proven to be, the most important and representative arts of the twentieth century, at a time when — he repeatedly points out — other commentators either undervalue them or misinterpret their special contribution by merely offering them up to values established by older forms of art and informed by earlier technologies.

Benjamin evaluated the strangely deadpan, matter–of–fact, depopulated photographs of Atget (images not made as art but as pragmatic aids to artists) by referring to a previous commentator who had interpreted them as looking like scenes of a crime.[6] This comment might be subtly connected with the statement by Paul Delaroche in 1839 that "from today painting is dead" (photography portrayed as a killer), as well as early debates as to whether the camera lies. All of which maps on to an illicit or disreputable reading of the photographic image, later found, as we have said, in Steyerl's "poor image" and also in Baudrillardian hyperbole wherein the photograph is implicitly evil because simulacral.[7] However, Benjamin does not offer any suggestion as to just what the crime or crimes suggested in Atget's photographs might be, instead bequeathing the question to future cultural gumshoes, including ourselves, to solve.

The Surrealists — who found value in Atget, as well as in the phenomena of atmosphere, the marvellous, and the

---

6. Benjamin, W. (1968). pp. 217–251.

7. O'Kane, P. (2014). Here I am again thinking of a Baudrillardian approach, most unlike my own more 'romantic', 'good' (in the Platonic sense) and virtuous approach to photography as primarily light based, rather than primarily simulacral — as discussed in *Where Is That Light Now?*

outmoded — were nothing if not *avant–garde*, and yet, as we began to tease out above, we also discern in Surrealism strong traces of Romanticism. Atmosphere, though a mysterious sounding concept, has always referred to an embodied and affective relationship (including the meteorological one) between mind, body and environment. Byron, the Shelleys, Poe, Scott etc. may have been adept at conjuring atmospheres necessary to the fulfilment of their Romantic ends. However, given Benjamin's comments (above) on Rimbaud etc. we may be tempted to try and unpick the difference between a Surrealist and a Romantic atmosphere? Is a Surrealist atmosphere not fundamentally derived from and contingent upon technologies, including the technology of the city itself, the technology of a Freudian method, the technologies of photography, the 'exquisite corpse', automatism, cinema, technically meticulous oil–painting, montage, frottage etc? Benjamin also provides a brief list of his own atmospheric scenarios, culminating with:

"Godforsaken Sunday afternoons in the proletarian quarters of the great cities ... the first glance through the rain–blurred window of a new apartment..."

Meanwhile, the marvellous in Romanticism might allude to an unworldly state, a sublime view, a heightened state of mind accessible through dramatic fictions, exceptional poetics, and feats of imagination, but in Surrealism it necessarily occurs everywhere and anywhere and at any time. The world is casually but irretrievably inverted when night becomes day.

The outmoded refers, not so much to an ancient ruin or emotive trace of the Classical era, but rather to the most recent, local and quotidian past, which refuses to be crudely discarded by the accelerating forces of modernity, and on the contrary, grows in lustre, appeal and quantity the faster, the newer, the more modern we become. Encountering the ruins of Tintern Abbey might conjure Romantic sensibility for Wordsworth but Breton and Giacometti can purchase ruins for a few sous in the flea market. As Benjamin suggested above, a kind of immanence occurs where and when all experiences become revalued according to an *avant–garde* Surrealist paradigm.

Even in the terrible wake of WWl, a passion for some form of Romanticism persists (as if it is just too deeply, historically ingrained within, or shot–through modern culture) if only as something valued in an untimely manner as outmoded, yet current, or current precisely because it is outmoded.

For Surrealism, any object, even Romanticism itself, can be singled—out as vulnerable, in fear of neglect, and thus as compelling, rendered exceptional by the carelessness of voraciously advancing fashion, valued not for its novelty, nor simply for the purposes of nostalgia, but because of its untimely incongruity and discomfort.

The weird genius of Dali, the mad love of Breton, the strange sacred of Bataille, or the slow motion celebrated by Bunuel or Deren, all perpetuate a twisted[8] Romanticist sensibility, sustained as a perverse and provocative differential, to confront an era of increasing speed and technological bravura, guided by an increasingly secular and rational episteme. Romanticism is thus repeatedly re–fitted and retro–fitted for purpose, keeping up with, providing a human interface for, ever–changing technological experiences.

Traces of Romanticism lingering in Surrealism are easier to perceive than anywhere in DADA, and yet within DADA's irreverent and belligerent absurdities too we might at least discern a few scraps of Quixotic adventuring and again glimpse possible confirmation of the notion that the *avant–garde* may be no more or less than the modern manifestation of Romanticism. Meanwhile, any clear distinction we perceive between Dada and Surrealism, may be interpreted as arising from the body of Romanticism split asunder by the unbearable moral weight and unprecedented horrors loaded onto its form by WW1.

If Atget, even before the turn of the century, presciently, reflectively and unconsciously revealed the backdrop to modern life to be a criminal context (the scene of a crime), it was perhaps certain illicit and illegitimate conditions (war, slavery, enclosure and exploitation, the insult and ugliness of industrialisation etc.) required to make the innovations of modernity possible. Under Benjamin's gaze these are confirmed as "evidence" and — we might

---

8. Or, perhaps 'blackened', following Andre Breton's coining of the term 'black humour'.

assume — "documents of barbarism".[9]

The future is forced to ease, edge, trick or barge its way into the present, often appearing brash, lawless, tasteless — *l'arriviste par excellence*. Not only do we fail or refuse to acknowledge, recognise, value, aestheticise or celebrate the future when it appears, we (out of fear, envy, and spite perhaps) keep it waiting, hoping it will remove or at least wipe its shoes — filthy with their newness — before entering.

And yet, as Benjamin so poetically and profoundly says in his *Theses on a Philosophy of History*: "Our coming was expected on earth".[10] Hence, youth, invariably, necessarily uncomfortable, misunderstood, rebellious, disruptive and even incomprehensible, is, despite all objections, inexorably destined to inherit and ultimately be accepted into polite discourse and established structures. Hence the new media, of Benjamin's day or of our own, gradually integrate and are integrated, eventually becoming the new norm where once they were only shockingly, offensively new.

Thus far we have connected, or attempted to connect, Wordsworth to Benjamin and Breton, and on to Steyerl as a contemporary commentator whose affirmation of poor images is surely a means by which to romantically affirm them as embodying a vulnerable, yet disruptive, innovative, illicit, piratic, and therefore potentially *avant–garde*

9.   Benjamin, W. (1968). pp. 253–264.
10. Benjamin, W. (1968). pp. 253–264.

agency. We might then justifiably recall that Coleridge and Wordsworth did not only excuse and explain their (innovative and transgressive) style and method but also the *content* of their poems which included references to the least privileged, the itinerant, the mentally disabled and, in various ways, marginal, un–empowered, and poor.

Similarly, Benjamin championed the image of the rag picker alongside the more aristocratic *flâneur*, and simultaneously promoted Charlie Chaplin's tramp as a figure of important cultural and political study, a prime example by means of which to illustrate Benjamin's innovative evaluation of cinema as an art of the crowd, of the mass, and again, of the poor.

Chaplin managed to make society's greatest loser into the world's best–known cinematic figure, and himself into the biggest star, at least as famous as any political or religious leader, any great thinker, artist, writer, scientist or sporting champion. Chaplin's tramp explores the new world of modernity (via the sets, lots, streets and outskirts of Los Angeles) exposing its inherent and potential absurdities while confronting all with the new emotion[11] of a deadpan, face–to–camera expression, presumably derived from long–established circus and music–hall routines, yet which seems somehow ripe for modernity and cinema.

Technology and romance may be connected by a sense in

11. Baudelaire, C. (1992). pp. 104–107. New emotions are subtly alluded to by Baudelaire in *Of The Heroism of Modern Life* within a list of updated attitudes and attributes required of a modern bourgeoisie emerging in 1840s Paris.

which both insist upon progress and narrative, but they are also connected by the risk, drama, the very unlikeliness of their respective aims and achievements, by the illicit, unstructured realm of adventure, and the unlikely possibility required for both to germinate and bloom.[12] From pirates to Pirate Radio, to pirated DVDs, from rogue knight to cheeky tramp, punk, or hacker, the risk–taking Romantic continues to occupy an illegitimate, lawless, necessarily out–on–a–limb and *avant–garde* position at the limits or margins of established culture, and even at the limits and margins of progressive and *emerging* culture.

Perhaps we could claim then that, while the *avant–garde* — along with certain romantic notions of resistance and possibility — may appear to die, its immaterial spirit or underlying motive persists as a necessary and intrinsic function of unfolding modernity, even reappearing in unexpected or apparently contradictory twists and guises but invariably in response to some techno–social advance. Hence today we again call, and always call an *avant–garde* to urgent action. As well as Don Quixote, the *flâneur*, Charlie Chaplin's on–screen tramp, the punk etc., an *avant–garde* re–emerges as, or alongside, new heroes and anti–heroes like the geeky, nerdy, isolated and hyper–technologised *otaku* teenager of 1980s Tokyo, described by German sociologist Volker Grassmuck in his 1990 essay *"I'm Alone, But Not Lonely".*[13]

---

12. Coyne, R. (1999). The image of a certain, now famous garage, in which Steve Jobs and other originators of the Silicon Valley phenomenon first regularly met, might here suggests itself.

13. Grassmuck, V. (2016).

Today's technologies, invariably, if inadvertently, perpetuate and extend the legacies of both Romanticism and the *avant–garde* by radicalising global communities and rousing a worldwide acceleration of cultural exchange which is inherently revolutionary, even as and if this progressive force is also opposed by increasingly extreme and rising forms of conservatism and fundamentalism that seem to welcome and exploit, yet contradict and refute, technology's promise of a more modern, global, transparent and potentially super–democratic form of political power.

Our unprecedented global collectivity and connectivity continues to entertain and amaze us, but we must urgently question what is happening to the social bonds that thus–far made modern social and political progress possible? Are they being usurped or outstripped by the prioritisation of just one kind or aspect of modern progress, i.e. technological progress? And if so might we need to look back into the roots of modern democracy, e.g. in revolutionary Romanticism, or perhaps the model of the satirical Swift–ean coffee house pamphleteer, to locate and reconnect with a proto–modern force that might infuse and temper a hyper–technologised society with more humane and affective, politically progressive and socially conscious visions and values? Currently, those values appear to be taken up, diverted, mediated, commodified and sold back to us for the price of our time and attention. What, therefore, is happening to our identities and relationships? Are we all *otaku* now?

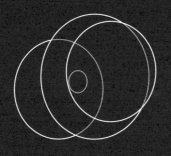

THE RED BLUSH
OF IRON

Politics may not be fundamentally technological but it is fundamentally human. Therefore, we might err if we invest too much in technology as a means by, and with which to solve human problems. Politics is people, politics is change, politics is tension, conflict and debate. Politics, we might summarise, is people interacting, and people are not zeros and ones, nor merely nodes, statistics or data (of which Benjamin and Kracauer had already grown suspicious by the 1920s and 30s).[1] Unlike data, people are, rather, a less quantifiable array of nervous responses to a changing environment, and an environment that people are changing. People are sensuous, fearful, ecstatic, lonely, angry, alienated, proud, abject, and at least as qualitative as they are quantitative.

Emoticons or *emojis* may become increasingly diverse in attempting to accurately portray a range of human feelings, however, they occupy an awkward overlap between our relatively aged humanity and the relatively youthful technology from which they have recently emerged. The ability of various technologies, and a history of technologies, to accurately translate or transmit emotion may be worth pursuing.

E.g. Vermeer portrayed seventeenth century Dutch women reading letters,[2] and though we can never know the content of those communications these placid scenes are sufficient to convey a certain touching humanity, a sense of quiet separation and human vulnerability implicating

---

1. Benjamin, W. (1968). p. 218., Kracauer, S. (1998)., and Kracauer, S. (1995).
2. Slive, S. (1995).

not only the technologies of letter writing but possibly those of shipping, navigation, map making, as well as oil painting techniques and contemporary developments in the preparation and use of lenses.

Charlie Chaplin, by merely gazing wistfully into a movie camera, made an emotional connection with millions worldwide, thus insisting that the latest technology, for his era, could be a useful vehicle for communicating nuances of emotion.

My own father's attempts, in the 1950s, to produce wistful and romantic–looking land and seascapes with his cheap Kodak camera are also testament to his generation's pursuit of a technologically assisted emotive and expressive amateur creativity.[3]

Meanwhile, professional photojournalism documenting the America–Vietnam War, is popularly believed to have provoked such significant shifting emotions as to initiate the beginnings of the end of that decades–old conflict. In that case, the emotion of shame, provoked and transmitted by the medium of photography, was seen as having power to change the American national moral narrative, or morale, heretofore driving the war along.

The emotive atmospheres captured by Atget around 1900 were also championed by both Benjamin and Surrealism as a means by which to picture, perpetuate and pursue

---

3. O'Kane, P. (2014). This alludes to a central theme to be found in previous **eeodo** publication *Where Is that Light Now?*

sacred, romantic and other pre–modern values, into and through our supposedly secular modernity.

In this list of examples, far from coldly distancing us from our emotions, new technology repeatedly proves itself to be a potential vehicle for emotion, perhaps even a vehicle that can rescue and breathe new life into a human emotional life that might otherwise be under threat from the very same technology. Heidegger optimistically quotes from Hölderlin: *"But where the danger is, grows / the saving power also"*.[4] Part of the aim and purpose of this book has been to test, explore and possibly reveal whether this quote remains true concerning current technologies? I.e. do they promise to rescue or cure as much as they appear to sting and to poison, our humanity, our society, our politics, our emotional life?[5]

Tanya Harrod, a British arts journalist who specialises in reviewing and monitoring the changing values of crafts, craftswomen and craftsmen, begins an essay with the words: "Emotional responses to materials have a long history…".[6] She goes on to speak of John Ruskin, as well as new media, and makes the valuable point (drawn from Ruskin) that the iron which is so symbolic of modernity in the late eighteenth and nineteenth centuries, and which captured Benjamin's attention as a symbol of modern

---

4. Heidegger, M. (1977). p.28.

5. Materials set aside for *Technologies of Romance* Part II include reflections on the pop music industry and the associations, positive and negative of the relationship between mass produced pop music, production lines and workaday lifestyles.

6. Harrod, T. (2015). pp. 327–340. *'Visionary Rather Than Practical': craft, art and material efficiency.*

transformation, is of the same stuff as that which gives red colouring to our blood and thus to our blushing cheek in moments of heightened emotion, involving fear, shame or anger. It is also the same substance that gives the planet Mars (associated, mythologically with our emotional life) its own ruddy hue. In this brief but poignant observation we can again see ways in which humanity and technology might empathise or homogeonise, rather than be seen as simply antagonistic.

Nevertheless, humanity might understandably feel both embarrassed and ashamed at the crude and short–sighted ways in which our enthusiasm for technologies has encouraged exploitation of the planet's minerals and other resources.

Contemporary photographer Edward Burtynsky,[7] in his museum–sized colour prints of mining zones, appears to sell some sense of this shame as a political value immersed within the aesthetics of a quasi–abstract art which is also a dystopian version of the landscape tradition. Landscape is something we readily associate with Romanticism, depicting a pre — or extra — urban idyll wherein we might hope to find relief and redemption from scenes of harsh urban modernity. But Burtynsky confronts us with a monstrous and dubious sublime, a representation of an awesome scene that may nevertheless be worthy of viewing, despite appearing inhospitable and even anathema to human life. His pictures might be said to illustrate the

7. Edward Burtynsky (http://www.edwardburtynsky.com/) is represented by Flowers gallery, London.

fundamental, yet largely hidden, chemical and mineral means by which we have achieved and sustained our much prized (and now formidably defended) modernity.

Coltan is a shamefully exploited, toxic material which has, in recent years, become hungrily sourced, collected, deployed and dumped in service of the lucrative and exponentially expansive smartphone industry for which it is a key component. From Burtynsky's and Harrod's viewpoint, the earth, the land and its resources are something with which we can either live empathetically or crudely exploit. The artists, craftsmen and craftswomen whom Harrod writes about might well be perceived as romantic for pursuing and perpetuating pre–modern traditions (albeit often in as contemporary a way as possible) and thus connecting or reconnecting us to pre–modernity or to earlier responses to modernity and industrialization (as suggested by reference to Ruskin, who in turn inevitably implicates William Morris). We might therefore feel justified in attempting to glean from the archives of an earlier state or stage of modernity, as well as within Romanticism itself, solutions and responses relevant to the technological surge that characterises our own era.

For Burtynsky the landscape is rendered cynically, a toxic territory, used and abused and probably exhausted of its value to modernity. And yet his photographs render this ecological crime scene (echoing Benjamin on Atget) strangely beautiful according to the traditions of modern, abstract art, and strangely bitter in relation to a bucolic tradition of Romantic natural beauty.

Frederick Jameson has cited a claim[8] that: "It is easier for mankind to contemplate the end of the world than to imagine the end of capitalism". If the planet we live on and depend upon is a resource exploited ruthlessly by modern technology to fuel a particular, modern society and economy (no longer based on rural subsistence and necessity but on urban and suburban, excessive and competitive consumption), then this fact haunts, embarrasses, and shames that same society while also threatening and intimidating it.

Climate change increasingly feels like a dystopian, sci–fi narrative coming all–too–true and all–too–soon, yet man is exploring the heavens and prospecting for further resources to exploit. If man continues to expansively explore and utilise, coming perhaps to even farm and mine other planets in economic rotations of thousands or millions of years, we notice in this scenario something unavoidably acquisitive and innately exploitative about man and his insatiably progressive relationship with nature and technology.

The Aboriginal Australians return to mind, as alternative representatives of man, said, in the citation that follows, to have no word for, or concept of progress, and whose original, fundamental and ultimate trajectory (if it can be described thus) is no more and no less than to maintain

---

8. The unattributed 'quote' appears in Jameson's article, *Future City* (*New Left Review*, 21, May–June 2003) within the following paragraph: "For it is the end of the world that is in question here... Someone once said that it is easier to imagine the end of the world than to imagine the end of capitalism. We can now revise that and witness the attempt to imagine capitalism by way of imagining the end of the world".

this world as it was at the moment of its creation.[9]

"In truth, as the anthropologist WEH Stanner long appreciated, the visionary realm of the Aborigines represents one of the great experiments in human thought. In place of technological wizardry, they invented a matrix of connectivity, an intricate web of social relations based on more than 100 named kin relationships. If they failed to embrace European notions of progress, it was not because they were savages, as the settlers assumed, but rather because in their intellectual universe, distilled in a devotional philosophy known as the Dreaming, there was no notion of linear progression whatsoever, no idealisation of the possibility or promise of change. There was no concept of past, present, or future. In not one of the hundreds of Aboriginal dialects and languages was there a word for time. The entire purpose of humanity was not to improve anything; it was to engage in the ritual and ceremonial activities deemed to be essential for the maintenance of the world precisely as it was at the moment of creation. Imagine if all of Western intellectual and scientific passion had focused from the beginning of time on keeping the Garden of Eden precisely as it was when Adam and Eve had their fateful conversation".

We only have to look at our sprawling, labyrinthine, choked, unplanned and almost uninhabitable modern cities to be forced to contemplate man's insatiably utilitarian, greedy, ignorant and short–sighted approach to economically manipulating its finite resources. No matter

9. From Wade Davis' review of *The World Until Yesterday* by Jared Diamond, The Guardian, 9th January, 2013. www.theguardian.com/books/2013/jan/09/history–society

how beautiful the world appears to man's avaricious and acquisitive eye, everything, it seems — including all forms of beauty — eventually becomes an exploitable economic resource and an expression of man's potential power over all that is not (and which is therefore deemed less than) man.

Heidegger's argument in *The Question Concerning Technology*[10] concerns itself with a historical level of technological change according to which a river like the Rhine (Heidegger's example), about which poets have been moved to write, may suffer the utilitarian indignity of being diverted and put to human use a by hydro–electric dam. Of course rivers have, for thousands of years been harnessed in various ways for their useful power, but Heidegger seems concerned that modern humanity may have crossed a line, perhaps in his own lifetime, or during the first industrial age — to which the Romantic movement responded. The crossing of this line has a profound impact and implications for modern society as a whole, and thus for anyone attempting to make art, a poem, or articulate a philosophy of Being, i.e. trying to locate and articulate our humanity by means of a modern response to nature as something simultaneously useful and beautiful, something both excellent and exploited.

The poetic relationship between humanity and nature has perhaps been broken, shifted, twisted or compromised by the extent to which technology now visibly renders nature useful, making a river into a machine, turning

10. Heidegger, M. (1977).

152

the awesome sublime into an extension of man.[11] Nevertheless, Hito Steyerl's witty twenty first century riposte, in a recently exhibited video *Liquidity Inc.* (2014)[12] suggests that we might also be able to think of machines as rivers according to a wider vision of the neoliberal economic and technological complex of global capitalism as a flow, wave or tsunami, and in response to which, she suggests, we can only follow martial artist and philosopher Bruce Lee's advice to "become water".

Deleuze & Guattari write: "A child in the dark, gripped with fear, comforts himself by singing under his breath".[13] Similarly, a bird sings, perhaps with joy, in fear, territorially, or to attract a mate. The same bird also carefully engineers its nest. As with the human so the animal, these different themes — what we might call the romantic and the technological — might underpin every life. In the narrative of a conscious existence, practical survival goes hand–in–hand with the expression and evaluation of that experience.

Heidegger wants to understand our relationship with technology and nature as a philosopher, but one who necessarily uses words that might be better, or best, wielded by poets, to whom he occasionally defers. Thus, influenced by Romanticism, while striving to articulate modernity, Heidegger understands language as a natural

---

11. McLuhan, M. (1994). Reference to Marshall McLuhan's title *Understanding Media: the extensions of man.*

12. Steyerl, H. (Artist). (2014).

13. Deleuze, G. & Guattari, F. (1996). *1837: Of The Refrain.* p. 311.

and not merely human technology. At worst, language distances us from, and merely represents nature. At best (at its most poetic) language integrates and reconnects us with everything that speaks.[14]

To what extent are we ourselves nature? To what extent are we natural extensions or parts of the natural world. To what degree are we ourselves technology or technological. Are we using the world or being used by it for its own inhuman purposes? Are nature and technology not merely outcomes of language after all, and is language then, as it constitutes a crucial interface with our environment, not itself a technology? If so we might call even poetry a technology and here begin to see technology and nature converge. Recall, Walter Benjamin claimed that technology availed us of a new or different nature, and it is perhaps within such ambiguities and convergences that what we call romance, Romanticism and technology meet, and see, and reflect upon each other.

14. Heidegger, M. (1982).

CONCLUSION

"Two things fill the mind with ever new and increasing admiration and awe, the more often and steadily we reflect upon them: the starry heavens above me and the moral law within me. I do not seek or conjecture either of them as if they were veiled obscurities or extravagances beyond the horizon of my vision; I see them before me and connect them immediately with the consciousness of my existence".[1]

As I write the final pages of this book, just before dawn on a winter morning in London, keeping me company are a fingernail moon and what is presumably a more distant, accompanying star. It is a classic, almost cartoon configuration, like something from a greetings card. I see this as an image, aesthetically, romantically perhaps, we might also say primitively, superstitiously and despite the fact that I am also inclined to see the scene more scientifically.

Despite appearances the moon does *not* have its own inner glow but merely reflects sunlight glancing over the earth, which, this morning, and from my perspective, leaves most of the moon in darkness and gives the impression that it is shaped like a fingernail (some call it a cuticle moon). The star that seems to be adjacent, as if neatly and pleasingly accompanying the moon, is in fact far distant, even though a form of empirical parallax makes it seem to share proximity with the moon.

Each of these ways of looking at my environment, the romantic and the scientific, the naively sensory and more

---

1.   Immanuel Kant's often quoted passage from the conclusion to *The Critique of Practical Reason*, 1788.

technically informed, nevertheless has its own truth and its own use for us. These two useful truths also enjoy a certain concurrence or convergence, if only because it is impossible to wholly prise our immediate, sensory view (informed by a history and culture of images) from the scientific facts that tell us that what we appear to see is not in fact or in truth what is there. Nevertheless, even a professional scientist cannot help but see the apparent configuration of star and moon as a charming image, neatly fulfilling a prescribed cultural example of a beautiful phenomenon.

We might argue that, just as we cannot and perhaps should not be constrained in playing–out and working through all of the possibilities and necessities of science, we should correspondingly respect and appreciate the possibilities and necessities of our sensory experience and consequently value, organise and analyse these according to something *other than* science — something we might call art.

Immanuel Kant, whom we inherit as an exemplary figure renowned for analytic rigour, insisted that the foundation of the Enlightenment's critical thinking was to investigate, think, and conclude for ourselves, having first presumed nothing concerning our object of enquiry. Furthermore, he found himself drawn, we might say beyond science into an artful accommodation of aesthetic judgement which he recognised as anomalous to his broader schema. This suggests that a satisfactory theorisation of art lies slightly beyond the powers of scientific and logical reasoning, leaving a certain vacuum within would–be omniscient Enlightenment thought, a space of uncertainty and possibility filled by the blossoming of those Romantics who followed on from and grew out of Kant's thought.

If we need a science of the senses then aesthetics has repeatedly attempted to provide one, however, it may ultimately be folly to set art before science as its object and its problem when these roles and positions might equally be reversed or reciprocated. Art, in the widest sense, may necessarily provide ways and means of representing science and apparently unscientific experience, as well as experience interpreted unscientifically. It may therefore incorporate or demand its own episteme, and one that is other to and critical of any episteme that prioritises the notion of knowledge.

Prior to our present epoch, in which we might consider science to be prioritised as a legitimate episteme, art and science were not always so clearly nor hierarchically distinct. E.g. in the image of the healer, the shaman, or even in the Aristotelian idea of art as cathartic[2] we discern combined and confused roots of art and science, artist and society. Those exceptions and anomalies, by means of which the senses and imagination might continue to challenge, exceed or diverge from science, also provoke the suggestion that science might be re–viewed from a primarily sensory and purposefully, even perversely, un–scientific perspective.

2.   Aristotle. (1987) and Aristotle. (1920).

Artists may attempt to turn science inside out by, for example suggesting that exceptions be given priority over rules — as posited by Alfred Jarry and his Pataphysics (defined as a science of exceptions).[3] A door also opens a little wider here into the radical and challenging theories of Gilles Deleuze and Felix Guattari.[4] Under the influence of the Romantic philosopher Friedrich Nietzsche they cultivated an anti–philosophical vocabulary diminishing any privilege awarded to organisation in scientific method. Deleuze & Guattari also promoted becomings over Being, and the model of animals and machines as extensions of our all–too–human understanding, just as Nietzsche himself had incorporated the superman into his expansive and speculative image of man as a becoming. Furthermore, Deleuze also pursued the provocative and playful title of his solo project *The Logic of Sense*,[5] a concept according to which the logic that is as crucial to science as its organisation comes under the power and scrutiny of the fickle, affective, unreasonable and disorganised senses.

Manuel Da Landa, an acolyte of Deleuze & Guattari's thought, has meanwhile determined their difficult concept 'A Body Without Organs' (drawn from the writings of Antonin Artaud) as comparable with a sky.[6] It may be worth recalling that Romantic artists too, cultivated a special relationship with the sky, climate, and a consequent

3. Jarry, A. (1992).

4. Deleuze, G. & Guattari, F. (1996).

5. Deleuze, G. (2003).

6. During his talk at the *Nature, Space, Society* series at Tate Modern, London (2004).

correspondence with emotion and inspiration. Whether it was Wordsworth's cloud, the turbulent sunsets and oceanic horizons of Turner and Caspar David Friedrich, or sparks of Romanticism lingering in Van Gogh's own firmament, correspondence between the sky and our emotional state is easy to locate through numerous examples of more or less Romantic painting, poetry and literature.

However, Da Landa offers an opportunity to perceive ourselves in Deleuzian terms as an eventful sky and thus 'A Body Without Organs'. Rather than consider ourselves a human subject, thereby delimiting our understanding to a relatively austere and all–too–organised Cartesian model, we might instead regard ourselves as a sky–like mass of volatile becomings, non–organised, swirling, baroque in their complexity and behaviours, eventful and intensive as opposed to existential and extensive.

Furthermore, Deleuze, in a short essay titled *A Philosophical Concept*… for Eduardo Cadaver's collection *Who Comes After The Subject?* (1991)[7] also suggested that an alternative to the subject might be accessed via the model of the event. He wrote:

"We wonder about what makes the individuality of an event: *a life, a season, a wind, a battle, 5 o'clock*…"**[8]**

In so doing he appears to equate the various events in this list, and thus a life becomes akin to a season or wind.

---

7.   Cadava, E., Connor, P. & Jean–Luc, N. (Eds.). (1991). pp. 94–95.

8.   Deleuze's italics.

Here, we seem to both disobey the priority and break the bounds of a scientific understanding and thereby perhaps gain access to some twenty first century equivalence of Romanticism, potentially an 'age of wonder'[9] in which art and science are not clearly, simply or confrontationally detached or opposed but mingled in rich discourse. A 'logic of sense', like a 'science of exceptions', purposefully gestures towards a realm of comprehension beyond art, beyond science and beyond any dualism or antagonism we might make of them or use to set them apart.

Modern technology, for all its welcome and wondrous gifts, becomes ugly or artless if led in certain directions, set to certain purposes, or taken to certain extremes. But such aesthetic judgements of the possibilities and tendencies of science, are based, not upon a scientific episteme but traceable to art's origins in, and influence upon moral as much as aesthetic values. Judgements of beauty or ugliness are inextricably related, not only to morality but also to the sublime, that fearful form of awe, laced with the sensual thrill of strange and dark sensations.

Aesthetic judgements of technologically progressive phenomena may provide checks and balances on science by insisting upon the primary human necessity to corral technology in service of the most rounded understanding of our full humanity, an understanding that accommodates art and aesthetic judgement without prioritising scientific, utilitarian or e.g. monetary value. Aesthetic judgements, which Kant stretched his reasoning to

9. Holmes, R. (2009).

accommodate, conceal within them the enduring vitality and validity of our most ancient questions, questions which may never expect to find unequivocal, logical, scientific or instrumental solutions but conjure sensual, affective, disorganised responses that may nevertheless prove strangely useful. They maintain their mysterious and non–instrumental value while nevertheless remaining precious, if not fundamental to our humanity.

Romanticism may have been a compensatory response to industrialisation, idealising nature and beauty as a salve to the ugliness of a new technology. However, as David Nye has shown, from industrialisation's earliest days modern man found beauty within new technology, admiring, fetishising, loving, first the grandiose scale of Fordist factories or illuminated iron bridges, now the quasi–religious hardware of our indispensable devices — the twenty first century equivalent of rosaries or worry beads.

So, which aspect of technology could we confidently judge and claim to be ugly? As Johan Grimonprez demonstrated in his innovative and provocative 1997 video essay *Dial H.I.S.T.O.R.Y*, the image of a crashing airliner only has to be slowed down and set to seductive disco music for it to become as pleasing as it is terrible.[10] As Nye also points out, the form of the exploding atom bomb became, for a generation at least, a strangely satisfactory image of sublime technology[11] embodying a macabre sense of human achievement. Even the most disturbing images

10. Grimonprez, J. (1997).

11. Nye, D. E. (1994).

of all — perhaps coarse B&W movie footage recording grim products of Nazi killing machines, or YouTube films showing the beheading of terrorist's hostages — yet lie on an uncomfortable threshold between a prohibited image and an image that all feel a need to see — perhaps out of base prurience, perhaps as a crucial aspect of our moral education.

In turning towards our own *dénouement* here, I switch–off my desk lamp the better to witness dawn breaking in the eastern sky. The sky responds, lighting–up pale blue. Thin clouds can be seen as if close to the crisp and clear moon. Switching off my light momentarily connects me back to Heidegger's or David Nye's images of a hydro–electric dam, though perhaps my lamp is connected to power from some more or less distant nuclear station.

The alarm on my smartphone, composed of synthetic musical imitations of nature, rings out. I silence it with a swipe across a much–thumbed screen, thinking briefly of the dubious morality of the coltan mineral crucial to the phone's functioning. I recall the point made by Tanya Harrod regarding the iron that formed much of the physical skeleton and infrastructure of our modernity; that also provided the war paint of Mars; and my all–too–visible, socially debilitating, adolescent blushes. I think of all the conscientious craftsmen and craftswomen championed by Harrod, who are sometimes (pejoratively) accused of being 'romantic' due to their noble affection for and dedication to experimentation with tradition, according to which they stay loyal to values of hapticity and knack in a virtual epoch wherein programmers have equalised a once far more diverse and specialised skills base.

The idiosyncratic and often personalised manipulations associated with craft cannot always be reduced to a scientific rationale, and thus become especially valued for the exceptional challenge they present to all that is mass–produced, all that is manufactured less humanely, lovingly, carefully, albeit to satisfy a perhaps less discerning, because less affluent market.

Nevertheless, a recent video by artist Elizabeth Price, titled simply *K* (2015),[12] uses digital animation techniques to describe the highly technologised, twenty first century mass production of lime green, gossamer–like stockings. The video leads us through the weaving of the yarn on a digitised loom and into the meticulous folding and packing of each individual item by a complex, light–fingered machine. Here there seems to be no question that we are enchanted by the artful and untimely gestures of an intricately elegant, computer–guided, aluminium, robotic mass–producer. We are seduced by the service it provides and even transported by the sight of it, just as we might by a dancer on a stage. Romance is right there in that gracious futurity, there in the subtle machinery, and yet, as with the hand–made values of craft, all this is inevitably informed by the past, as even here an unbroken tradition erupts into contemporary guise as the new.

The sky cracks and brightens. As a twenty first century commentator on these concerns I feel displaced,

12. Price, E. (Artist). (2015).

de–centered, and slightly daunted. The silhouettes of builders' cranes become visible against the horizon, red lights flash at their apex. Meanwhile twinkling jets cruise through a wash of purple sky shading into cyan. Each air-liner is delivering passengers to London and I imagine their perspective, cooped–up in a cramped and cosset-ed, all–too–conditioned space, hostages to a technology on which modern lives have come to depend. The gold-en or romantic age of aviation is gone, supplanted by ex-hausting experiences in alienating terminals, terror check shakedowns and the marketisation of every moment spent within the sterile bounds of an airport.

Perhaps the passengers, staring out of crumpled, long–hauled bodies, down into the sprawling city where I sit, nevertheless see me, at least as one dash of light among millions flickering below in the sublime city, soaked in its dawn gloom. Everywhere man is making, manipulating and endeavouring, everywhere venturing, forging and aspiring, all by technologised means, but nevertheless informed, guided, protected and redeemed by various forms of romance.

Today (and in Benjamin's and Heidegger's inter–war *milieu* too) technology appears to loom as large in our lives as any god ever did. It becomes our paradigm and episteme, that which we turn to for answers to almost every ques-tion. Our smartphones are often the last things we touch before retiring at night and the first thing we reach for on rising. But it seems necessary, crucial even, to temper and challenge, infuse and divert their (and *our*) myopia with reminders of a romance that persists as a human trait, a peculiarly human way of understanding experience and gleaning meaning from a life that we suspect will never be adequately explained by science, nor sufficiently served and serviced by technology alone.

Romance must never be imposed upon us but rather felt, wielded and guided according to our own needs as an intuitive and empowering agency. Technology should never stand unopposed and unconsidered from alternative perspectives. But what might a non–, anti–, post– or alter–technological position be? Perhaps that of what we have here called 'romance', and which might mean — Part I of this book having now been written — everything that technology is not and can never be, everything that, while it may contend with, grace, or compensate for technology, is precisely non–utilitarian, non–progressive, non–dynamic, non–modern, non–technical and non–exploitative.

Victims of manipulative, deceptive and destructive romances may object at this point. Anyone 'taken for a ride' or 'sold a story' by any kind of seducer, might argue that romance can indeed be both utilitarian and exploitative. My response might then be to distinguish any such *applied* romance from the more abstract and elusive agency or quality used throughout the preceding exploration, wherein romance retains the narrative form and force that allows us to survive ordeals and, despite them, rescue a meaningful life.

To conclude on a hopefully excusable, but current and politically urgent note, progressives and those on the political Left are, as I write, greatly intimidated and rightly appalled by the reckless way the political Right is playing with truth and fact for its own selfish and destructive ends. *Technologies of Romance* Part I hopefully provides elements of a way to respond, by e.g. advocating greater trust in the romantic roots of revolutionary and progressive thought, greater faith in a personal and collective hunch, greater belief in the way we recognize each other as comrades who also know, viscerally and innately, intuitively and unquestioningly what we believe to be right when we do come together as one; a kind of thinking, feeling and acting, based not only on science and technology but also on some more elusive and affective murmuration, the barely articulated, passionate and perhaps irrational intuition that ultimately drives a political movement rooted in a desire for peace, kindness, conscientiousness, inclusivity and social justice.

It may also be time for the Left to romantically imagine, to be passionate and inspired, to believe in a magic of its own, and — following Benjamin — to trust and value stories, over, above and in preference to data and information.

Having recorded this fleeting glimpse of clarity, I hope we have arrived together at some affirmative sense of the inspired trajectory (if not always precise aim) of this book, as well as a satisfactory, if temporary interpretation of the meaning of our title.

photocopy please (Bit larger?)

pls a
bit larger

- p. 15 and 16
- p. 168

- and front & back of
  handwritten notes

BIBLIOGRAPHY

Agamben, G. (2007). *Profanations*. (J. Fort, Trans.). New York : Zone Books.

Aristotle. (1920). *On the Art of Poetry*. Oxford : Oxford University Press.

Aristotle. (1987). *The Poetics of Aristotle*. (S. Halliwell, Trans.). London : Duckworth.

Banham, R. (1962). *Theory and Design in the First Machine Age*. London : The Architectural Press.

Bataille, G. (1991). *The Accursed Share: an essay on general economy*, volume I. (R. Hurley, Trans.). New York : Zone Books.

Bataille, G. (1993). *The Accursed Share: an essay on general economy*, volumes II & III. (R. Hurley, Trans.). New York : Zone Books.

Baudelaire, C. (1970). *Paris Spleen 1869*. (L. Varese, Trans.). New York : A New Directions Book.

Baudelaire, C. (1992). *Selected Writings on Art and Literature*. (P. E. Charvet, Trans.). London : Penguin Books.

Baudrillard, J. (1983). *Simulations*. (P. Foss, P. Patton & P. Beitchman, Trans.). New York : Semiotext, Inc.

Baudrillard, J. (1993). *The Transparency of Evil: essays on extreme phenomena*. (J. Benedict, Trans.). London : Verso.

Baudrillard, J. (1996). *The Perfect Prime*. (C. Turner, Trans.). London : Verso.

Baudrillard, J. (1998). *Selected Writings*. (M. Poster, Ed.). Cambridge, U.K. : Polity Press.

Baudrillard, J. (2012). *The Ecstasy of Communication*. Cambridge, Mass. & London : Semiotext(e).

Baume, N. (2005). *Getting Emotional*. Boston : Institute of Contemporary Art.

Beedham, M. (2010). *The Novels of Kazuo Ishiguro*. U.K. : Palgrave Macmillan.

Benjamin, W. (1968). *Illuminations: essays and reflections*. (H. Arendt, Ed.). (H. Zohn, Trans.). New York : Schocken Books.

Benjamin, W. (1973). *Charles Baudelaire: a lyric poet in the era of high capitalism*. (H. Zohn, Trans.). London : NLB.

Benjamin, W. (1978). *Reflections: essays, aphorisms, autobiographical writings*. (E. Jephcott, Trans.). New York : Schocken Books.

Benjamin, W. (1985). *Moscow Diary*. (R. Sieburth, Trans.). (G. Smith, Ed.). U.S.A. : MIT Press.

Benjamin, W. (1999). *The Origin of German Tragic Drama*. (J. Osborne, Trans.). London & New York : Verso.

Benjamin, W. (2000). *One–Way Street and Other Writings*. (E. Jephcott, & K. Shorter, Trans.). London & New York : Verso.

Benjamin, W. (2003). *The Arcades Project*. (H. Eiland, & K. McLaughlin, Eds). U.S.A. & England : The Belknap Press of Harvard University Press.

Benjamin, W. (2004). *Walter Benjamin: selected writings: volume I, 1913–1926*. (M. Bullock, & M.W. Jennings, Eds.). U.S.A. & England : The Belknap Press of Harvard University Press.

Benjamin, W. (2016). *The Storyteller: tales out of loneliness*. (S. Dolbear, E. Leslie & S. Truskolaski, Trans. & Eds.). London & New York : Verso.

Bonanos, C. (2012). *Instant: the story of Polaroid*. New York : Princeton Architectural Press.

Borges, J. L. (1964). *Labyrinths: selected stories & other writings*. (D. A. Yates & J. E. Irby, Eds.). New York : A New Directions Book.

Borges, J. L. (2000). *Fictions*. (A. Hurler, Trans.). London : Penguin Books.

Borges, J. L. (2002). *The Book of Imaginary Beings*. (N. T. di. Giovanni, Trans.). London : Vintage.

Bourriaud, N. (Ed.). (2009). *Tate Triennial*. London : Tate Publishing.

Boyer, J. (Ed.). (2013). *This Me of Mine: self, time & context in the digital age*. London : XLIBRIS.

Buck–Morss, S. (1989). *The Dialectics of Seeing: Walter Benjamin and the arcades project*. Mass. & London : MIT Press.

Brecht, B. (2003). *Brecht on Art and Politics*. (T. Kuhn, & S. Giles, Eds.). (L. Bradley, S. Giles & T. Kuhn, Trans.). London : Methuen.

Breton, A. (1987). *Mad love*. (M. A. Caws, Trans.). Lincoln, Neb. & London : University of Nebraska Press.

Breton, A. (2007). *Nadja*. Paris : Gallimard.

Burke, E. (1998). *A Philosophical Enquiry Into the Origins of Our Ideas of the Sublime and Beautiful*. (A. Phillips, Ed.). Oxford : Oxford University Press.

Burley, R. (2013). *The Disappearance Of Darkness: photography at the end of the analog era*. New York : Princeton Architectural Press.

Cadava, E., Connor, P. & Jean–Luc, N. (Eds.). (1991). *Who Comes After the Subject?*. London : Routledge.

Canetti, E. (1992). *Crowds and Power*. (C. Stewart, Trans.). Harmondsworth : Penguin Books.

Caygill, H. (1995). *A Kant Dictionary*. England : Blackwell.

Caygill, H. (1998). *Walter Benjamin: the colour of experience*. London & New York : Routledge.

Cervantes, M. de. (1950). *The Adventures of Don Quixote*. (J. M. Gohen, Trans.). London : Penguin Books.

Clare, J. (2007). *John Clare: poems selected by Paul Farley*. England : Faber and Faber.

Clark, T. J. (2003). *The Painting of Modern Life: Paris in the art of Manet and his followers*. London : Thames & Hudson.

Coleridge, S. T. (2006). *Samuel Taylor Coleridge: poems selected by James Fenton*. England : Faber and Faber.

Columpar, C. & Mayer, S. (2009). *There She Goes: feminist filmmaking and beyond*. Detroit : Wayne State University Press.

Costelloe, T. M. (Ed.). (2012). *The Sublime: from antiquity to the present*. Cambridge : Cambridge University Press.

Coyne, R. (1999). *Technoromanticism: digital narrative, holism, and the romance of the real*. U.S.A. : MIT Press.

Crane, D., Hebron, S. & Woof, R. (Entries). (2002). *Romantics & Revolutionaries: regency portraits from the National Portrait Gallery London*. London : National Portrait Gallery.

Damrosch, L. (2013). *Jonathan Swift: his life and his world*. New Haven & London : Yale University Press.

Danow, D. K. (1995). *The Spirit of Carnival: magical realism and the grotesque*. Lexington, Ky. : University Press of Kentucky.

Deleuze, G. & Guattari, F. (1996). *A Thousand Plateaus: capitalism and schizophrenia*. (B. Massumi, Trans.). London : The Athlone Press.

Deleuze, G. (2003). *The Logic of Sense*. (M. Lester, Trans.). (C. V. Boundas, Ed.). London : Continuum.

Dillon, B. (Ed.). (2011). *Ruins*. London : Whitechapel Gallery & Cambridge, Mass. : MIT Press.

Doyle, J. (2013). *Hold It Against Me: difficulty and emotion in contemporary art*. Durham, NCU & London : Duke University Press.

Duras, M. (1986). *The Malady of Death*. (B. Bray, Trans.). New York : Grove Press, Inc.

Duras, M. (2006). *The Lover*. (B. Bray, Trans.). London, New York, Toronto & Sydney: Harper Perennial.

Edgerton, D. (2008). *The Shock of The Old*. London : Profile Books.

Edensor, T. (2005). *Industrial Ruins: space, aesthetics and materiality*. Oxford : Berg.

Eliot, T. S. (1981). *The Waste Land, and Other Poems*. London : Faber & Faber.

Fletcher, J. & Calder, J. (Eds.). (1986). *The Nouveau Roman Reader*. London : Calder.

Gleber, A. (1999). *The Art of Taking A Walk: flanerie, literature, and film in Weimar culture*. New Jersey : Princeton University Press.

Golding, S. (1997). *The Eight Technologies of Otherness*. London & New York : Routledge.

Grassmuck, V. (2016). "I'm Alone, But Not Lonely". London : eeodo.

Hart, S. M. & Wen–chin Ouyang, W–c (Eds.). (2010). *A Companion to Magical Realism*. Woodbridge : Tamesis.

Hanssen, B. & Benjamin, A. (Eds.). (2002). *Walter Benjamin and Romanticism*. New York & London : Continuum.

Harrod, T. (2015). *The Real Thing: essays on making in the modern world*. London : Hyphen Press.

Hatherley, O. (2010). *A Guide to the New Ruins of Great Britain*. London : Verso.

Heidegger, M. (1977). *The Question Concerning Technology and Other Essays*. (W. Lovitt, Trans.). New York, London, Toronto & Sydney : Harper Perennial.

Heidegger, M. (1982). *On the Way to Language*. (P. D. Hertz, Trans.). San Francisco : Harper and Row.

Heidegger, M. (1993). *Basic Writings: from Being and Time (1927) to The Task of Thinking (1964)*. (D. F. Krell, Ed.). Abingdon : Routledge.

Heidegger, M. (2001). *Being And Time*. (J. Macquarrie & E. Robinson, Trans.). U.K. & U.S.A. : Blackwell.

Hell, J. & Schönle, A. (Eds.). (2010). *Ruins of Modernity*. Durham, N.C. & London : Duke University Press.

Hiltunen, A. (2002). *Aristotle in Hollywood: the anatomy of successful storytelling*. Bristol : Intellect Books.

Hoberman, J. (2012). *Film After Film: or, what became of twenty first century cinema?*. Brooklyn, N.Y. : Verso.

Holmes, R. (2009). *The Age of Wonder: how the Romantic generation discovered the beauty and terror of science*. London : Harper Press.

Ishiguro, K. (2016). *The Buried Giant*. London : Faber & Faber, 2016.

Jarry, A. (1992). *Adventures in 'Pataphysics: collected works I*. (P. Edwards & A. Melville, Trans.). London : Atlas.

John Eakin, P. (2008). *Living Autobiographically: how we create identity in narrative*. U.S.A. & London : Cornell University Press.

Jonscher, C. (2000). *WiredLife: who are we in the digital age?*. London : Anchor.

Judt, T. (2005). *Postwar: a history of Europe since 1945*. London: Pimlico Random House.

Kant, I. (1987). *Critique of Judgment*. (W. S. Pluhar, Trans.). Indianapolis, Cambridge : Hackett Publishing Company.

Kant, I. (1991). *Observations on the Feeling of the Beautiful and Sublime*. (J. T. Goldthwait, Trans.). Berkeley, Los Angeles & London : University of California Press.

Kholeif, O. (Ed.). (2015). *You Are Here — Art After the Internet*. Manchster, England : Cornerhouse.

Kittler, F. A. (1999). *Gramophone, Film, Typewriter*. (G. Winthrop–Young & M. Wutz, Trans.). U.S.A. : Stanford University Press.

Kracauer, S. (1995). *The Mass Ornament: Weimar essays*. (T. Y. Levin, Trans. & Ed.). U.S.A. & England : Harvard University Press.

Kracauer, S. (1998). *The Salaried Masses: duty and distraction in Weimar Germany*. (Q. Hoare, Trans.). London & New York : Verso.

Krause, L. & Petro, P. (Eds.). (2003). *Global Cities: cinema, architecture, and urbanism in a digital age*. New Brunswick, N.J. & London : Rutgers University Press.

Leakey, F. W. (1992). *Baudelaire, Les Fleurs du Mal*. Cambridge : Cambridge University Press.

Levinson, P. (2003). *Real Space: the fate of physical presence in the digital age, on and off planet*. London : Routledge.

Lyons, M. C. (Trans.). (2008). *The Arabian Nights, Tales of 1001 Nights, volume I, nights 1 to 294*. London : Penguin Books.

Marchand, Y. & Meffre, R. (2010). *The Ruins of Detroit*. Göttingen : Steidl.

Marcus, G. (2001). *Lipstick Traces: a secret history of the twentieth century*. London : Faber and Faber.

Matthews, S. & Groes, S. (Eds.). (2009). *Kazuo Ishiguro*. London : Continuum.

McLuhan, M. (1994). *Understanding Media: the extensions of man*. U.S.A. : MIT Press.

McQuillan, M. (2005). *The Narrative Reader*. London & New York : Routledge.

Mishima, Y. (2000). *The Sound of Waves*. London : Vintage.

Mishima, Y. (2000). *The Sailor Who Fell from Grace With the Sea*. London : Vintage.

Mishima, Y. (2001). *The Temple of the Golden Pavilion*. London : Vintage.

Mumford, L. (1934). *Technics and Civilization*. London : Routledge.

Mumford, L. (1991). *The City in History: its origins, its transformations, and its prospects*. London : Penguin Books.

Murakami, H. (2007). *Blind Willow, Sleeping Women*. London : Vintage.

Nietzsche, F. (1969). *Thus Spoke Zarathustra: a book for everyone and no one*. (R. J. Hollingdale, Trans.). London : Penguin Books.

Nietzsche, F. (1990). *Twilight of The Idols and the Anti—Christ*. (R. J. Hollingdale, Trans.). London : Penguin Books.

Nietzsche, F. (2001). *The Gay Science*. (B. Williams, Ed.). (J. Nauckhoff, Trans.). (A. D. Caro, Poems Trans.). U.K. : Cambridge University Press.

Nochlin, L. (2001). *The Body In Pieces: the fragment as a metaphor of modernity*. London : Thames & Hudson.

Nye, D. E. (1994). *American Technological Sublime*. U.S.A. : MIT Press.

O'Kane, P. (2014). *Where Is That Light Now?*. London : eeodo

Ostrowska, D. (2008). *Reading the French New Wave: critics, writers and art cinema in France*. London : Wallflower.

Pascal, B. (1995). *Pensees*. London : Penguin Books.

Pawley, M. (1990). *Theory and Design in The Second Machine Age*. Oxford : Basil Blackwell.

Perron, B. & Wolf, M. J. P. (Eds.). (2009). *The Video Game Theory Reader 2*. New York : Routledge.

Poe, E. A. (1986). *The Fall of the House of Usher and Other Stories*. London : Marshall Cavendish Partworks.

Réda, J. (1996). *The Ruins of Paris*. (M. Treharne, Trans.). London : Reaktion.

Riesman, D. (2001). *The Lonely Crowd: a study of the changing American character*. New Haven & London : Yale University Press.

Robbe—Grillet, A. (1965). *Two Novels by Robbe—Grillet: Jealousy and In The Labyrinth*. New York : Grove Press, Inc.

Roe, N. (Ed.). (2005). *Romanticism: an Oxford guide*. Oxford : Oxford University Press.

Roman, M. (2016). *On Stage: the theatrical dimension of video image*. England : Intellect.

Rush, F. (Ed.). (2004). *The Cambridge Companion to Critical Theory*. U.K. : Cambridge University Press.

Sargent, E. (Ed.). (2012). *Superhuman: exploring human enhancement from 600 BCE to 2050*. London : Wellcome Collection.

Sebald, W. G. (2001). *Austerlitz*. (A. Bell, Trans.). London : Penguin Books.

Sebald, W. G. (2002). *The Rings of Saturn*. (M. Hulse, Trans.). London : Vintage.

Shakespeare, W. (2004). *Othello*. London : The Arden Shakespeare.

Shelley, M. (2003). *Frankenstein: or, The Modern Prometheus*. London & New York : Penguin Books.

Slive, S. (1995). *Dutch Painting 1600–1800*. New Haven & London : Yale University Press.

Song, B. (2015). *Cash or Smash*. London : eeodo.

Stafford, F. (2013). *Lyrical Ballads: 1798 and 1802: William Wordsworth and Samuel Taylor Coleridge*. Oxford : Oxford University Press.

Steyerl, H. (2012). *The Wretched of the Screen*. Berlin : Sternberg Press.

Streeter, T. (2011). *The Net Effect*. New York & London : New York University Press.

Sutton, D., Brind, S. & McKenzie, R. (Eds). (2007). *The State of the Real: aesthetics in the digital age*. London : I.B. Tauris.

Swift, J. (2003). *Gulliver's Travels*. London : Penguin Books.

Tronzo, W. (Ed.). (2009). *The Fragment: an incomplete history*. Los Angeles, Calif. : Getty Research Institute.

Turkle, S. (1995). *Identity In the Age of the Internet*. New York & England : Simon & Schuster.

Turkle, S. (2008). (Ed.) *The Inner History of Devices*. New York : Routledge.

Turkle, S. (2011). *Alone Together: why we expect more from technology and less from each other*. New York : Basic Books.

Whitehead, A. N. (1943). *Adventures of Ideas*. England : Cambridge University Press.

Wiedmann, A. K. (1979). *Romantic Roots in Modern Art: romanticism and expressionism: a study in comparative aesthetics*. Old Woking : Gresham Books.

Willett, J. (1996). *Art and Politics in the Weimar Period: the new sobriety, 1917–1933*. New York : Da Capo Press.

Witkin, R. W. (2003). *Adorno on Popular Culture*. London : Routledge.

Wordsworth, W. (2001). *William Wordsworth: poems selected by Seamus Heaney.* England : Faber & Faber.

Zamora, L. P. & Wendy B. Faris, W. B. (Eds.). (1995). *Magical Realism: theory, history, community.* Durham, N.C. : Duke University Press.

MOVING IMAGE/ MUSIC

Bresson, R. (Director). (1983). *L'Argent.* (Film). (H. Jean–Marc, Producer). France & Switzerland.

Fei, C. (Artist). (2006). *Whose Utopia?.* (Film). China.

Coen J. (Director). (1996). *Fargo.* (E. Coen, Producer). (Film). U.S.A. & U. K. : PolyGram Filmed.

Cousins, M. (Director). (2012). *The Story of Film: an odyssey.* (Film). U.K.

Grimonprez, J. (Director). (1997). *Dial H.I.S.T.O.R.Y* (Film). (J. Grimonprez, Producer). England : Zap–O–Matik.

Hitchcock, A. (Director). (1954). *Dial M for Murder.* (Film). U.S.A.

Holdsworth, J. (Director & Producer). (2013). *No Sex Please We're Japanese.* (T.V.). U.K.

Kiarostami, A. (Director). (2002). *TEN.* (Film). Iran.

Leigh, M. (Director). (1993). *Naked.* (Film). (S. C. Williams, Producer). England : Thin Man Films.

Morrison, V. (1970). *Moondance.* (Music Album). (L. Merenstein & V. Morrison, Producers). New York.

Morrison, V. (1979). *Into the Music.* (Music Album). (V. Morrison & M. Glossop, Producers). U.S.A. & U.K.

Price, E. (Artist). (2015). *K.* (Film). London.

Spielberg, S. (Director). (1977). *Close Encounters of the Third Kind.* (J. Phillips & M. Phillips, Producers). (Film). U.S.A. : EMI Films.

Stone, O. (Director). (1987). *Wall Street.* (E. R. Pressman, Producer). (Film). U.S.A. : Amercent Films.

Steyerl, H. (Artist). (2014). *Liquidity Inc.* (Film). Berlin.

Vertov, D. (2000). *Man with a Movie Camera* (Film). U.K. : BFI.

Zellner, D. (Director). (2014). *Kumiko, the Treasure Hunter.* (Film). U.S.A. : Ad Hominen Enterprised & Lila 9th Productions.

ABOUT THE AUTHORS

Paul O'Kane is an artist, writer and lecturer in Critical Studies, Fine Art at Central Saint Martins College, University of the Arts London. His main research interests are: technology, history, Romanticism, modernity, photography and film. Paul O'Kane writes for leading art journals including *Art Monthly* and *Third Text* and is a member of AICA (International Association of Art Critics).

Howard Caygill is a renowned thinker, writer and lecturer on History and Philosophy. He is Professor of Modern European Philosophy at Kingston University, London and has published the following books: *A Kant Dictionary* (1995), *Introducing Walter Benjamin* (1994), *Levinas and The Political* (2001), *On Resistance* (2013), *Walter Benjamin and the Colour of Experience* (1998). Caygill is currently preparing a new publication, *Kafka: In The Light Of The Accident* (2017).

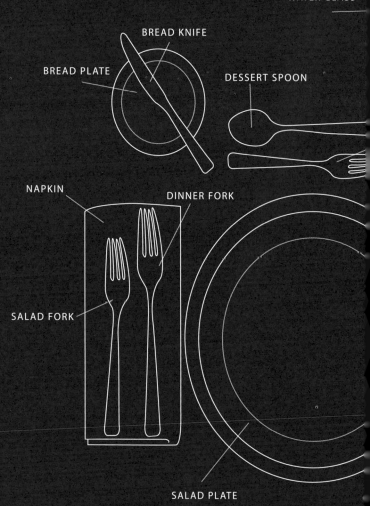

WATER GLASS

BREAD KNIFE

BREAD PLATE

DESSERT SPOON

NAPKIN

DINNER FORK

SALAD FORK

SALAD PLATE

RED WINE GLASS

ORK

TEASPOON

WHITE WINE GLASS

SOUP SPOON

TEACUP AND SAUCER

ABOUT THE ILLUSTRATIONS

Luna Sun is a recent graduate of Visual Communications, London College of Communication, UAL. She is based in Taipei and NYC (www.lunasun.co.uk) specialising in stationery design. Luna provided the drawing that we deployed on the cover and deconstructed and dispersed throughout this book. It is also presented in full on pages 184–185. What we came to refer to as the 'Dinner Service' drawing was made in October 2015 in response to a project titled: *How can publication design help impart dining etiquettes to business professionals?* It was constructed using photography, vector illustration and digital printing. Originally it was displayed both as an A3 drawing and as part of a hand–bound book.

The photograph on pages 180–181 is *Carousel* (2002) by Paul O'Kane. It was deployed as the lead image for our Indiegogo crowdfunding appeal and other events related to this book's launch and promotion.

ABOUT EEODO

eeodo is a fledgling nonprofit publisher making artists' books. While supporting invention and speculation, we are committed to developing a broad audience and promoting the idea that art, whilst innovative and esoteric is also an everyday human exchange.

Our previous books include:
Where is That Light Now? (2014) by Paul O'Kane
Cash or Smash (2015) by Bada Song
"I'm Alone, But Not Lonely" (2016) by Volker Grassmuck

eeodo is Bada Song, Barnaby Lambert & Paul O'Kane.

EEODO USED INDIEGOGO'S CROWDFUND-
ING PLATFORM TO RAISE PART OF THE
COST OF THIS BOOK. ALL CONTRIBUTORS'
NAMES ARE PRINTED HERE AS A LASTING
RECORD OF OUR GRATITUDE.

Sanaz Amidi

Tom Anholt

Cathy Bradley

Eleanor Vonne Brown

Scarlett Brunell

Sonia Cabrera

Dickie Cohen

Joshua Crowle

Deirdre Daly

Steve Dowson

Gillian Duffy

Tatjana Gretschmann

Harriet Hill

Jean Humphreys

John Humphreys

Tom Kemp

Sarah Knill-Jones

Maureen Lambert

Amanda Lambert

Anthony Lambert

David Lambert

Carmen Lamberti

Barry Leary

Shireen Liane

Eric Michel

Elaine Mullings

Mike O'Kane

Sonya Park

Emma Skeldon

Sammy Stevens

Lexi Stones

John Whapham

Poppy Whatmore

Kyle Zeto

Andrew Baker

Nicholas Baldion

Michele Beadle

Jasmine Brunell

Noriko Hasuno

John Koestle-Cate

Lucy Large

Xenia Lonergan

Unmi Li

Carol Misch

Richard Moon

Rom Nom

Margot Peters

Georgina Sleap

Alexia Synodinou

Maria Theodoraki

Daniel Ward

Alex Hanna

Georgia Korossi

TECHNOLOGIES OF ROMANCE – PART I
by Paul O'Kane

Main Text © 2017 by **Paul O'Kane**
Preface © 2017 by **Howard Caygill**
Illustrations © 2015 by **Luna Sun**

Published by **eeodo**
© 2017 All rights reserved

Flat 3 Collingwood House
3 Cottage Green
London SE5 7ST

www.eeodo.co.uk

Conceived, Designed & Edited by **eeodo**
Typographic & Technical Design by **Barnaby Lambert**
Illustrations by **Luna Sun**

Printed by the Print Studio at London Collage
of Communication, University of the Arts London

Limited edition of 500

ISBN: 978–0–9929857–3–8

ual:

Supported using public funding by
**ARTS COUNCIL
ENGLAND**

LOTTERY FUNDED

Speaking English